MEN OF ALDRIDGE

A LOCAL HISTORY OF THE AREA NOW INCLUDED IN THE URBAN DISTRICT OF ALDRIDGE

by

JIM GOULD, M.A., F.S.A.

ALAN SUTTON

1983

Alan Sutton Publishing Limited
17a Brunswick Road
Gloucester GL1 1HG

First published 1957
Reprinted with additions 1983
Copyright © 1983 Jim Gould

British Library Cataloguing in Publication Data

Gould, James
  Men of Aldridge—2nd ed.
  1.   **Aldridge (Staffordshire)—History**
  I.   **Title**
  942.4'92   DA690.A/

  ISBN 0 086299 058 0

Printed in Great Britain
by Redwood Burn Limited, Trowbridge

MEN OF ALDRIDGE

The Parish Church, Aldridge

FOREWORD

Parish and local histories have long been a love of the English nation. All add things of interest to the national picture. All involve years of research and the accumulation of much material. In only a few is this vast mass of fact reduced to a balance between information and readability.

In this history of Aldridge, an area torn between growing manu- factures and the dormitory dwellings of Birmingham and Black Country workers, I believe that the author has succeeded in placing the local facts against the historical background in a well digested manner which can be assimilated by both the general reader and the student. He covers the whole field of human activity in the area from the scraps of flint tools on the surface to the growth of factories. He has not forgotten the humanities and his gleanings from the adminis- tration of the Poor Law in the eighteenth century read like summaries of Dickens' plots.

I find delightful that he has abstained from long genealogies, from detailed and tedious notes of minute observations in church architec- ture. He writes of people speaking across the past from the fragments of documents left almost by accident or the marks and traces of the human hand in the field.

As a study of a sparsely inhabited area in the Midland forest belt I am sure that this work will fill a need for those who like to teach or learn history from a human angle.

A. H. OSWALD, M.A., F.S.A., F.M.A.

To DOROTHY

who has suffered much from too many papers
too often left in too many places, but who yet
refrained from too frequent
attempts to straighten
them.

PREFACE TO THE REPRINT

In issuing this reprint of *Men of Aldridge*, I would like to have made
some alterations, but the need to keep down costs prohibits this.
However it has been possible to include as an appendix, a copy of a
more recent paper that appeared in the *Transactions of the South
Staffordshire Archaeological and Historical Society*. This modifies some
of the details in the earlier book. Further details have also appeared in
Transactions of that society. In volume 7 (pages 21–39) are more
details of the forest, in volume 11 (pages 58–66) are details of the
medieval ironworks at Bourne Pool, whilst in volume 18, pages 47
to 52 refer to Aldridge church. The same volume (pages 1 to 28)
contains the findings of Mr. S.R. Jones and Mr. V.F. Penn on the
cruck-house that once stood in High St. Mr. Alan Saville's reconsideration of the Bourne Pool flints is in volume 14, pages 6 to 28.

JIM GOULD

Aldridge, December 1982

PREFACE

In writing this story of Aldridge I have received help from many people. I am indebted to the staff of the Birmingham Reference Library who, with patience, made available the documents and books that are in their keeping ; Mr. Stitt and Miss Gollancz were also helpful, making accessible the many records that are in the County Record Office and the William Salt Library. Mr. F. Price, the Walsall Librarian, in addition to the help he gave as Librarian, also added a generous helping of personal encouragement. The Rector of Aldridge, and the Vicar of Great Barr, freely allowed me to study the Registers and other documents that are in their possession, both being most co-operative. Mention must also be made of Mr. J. Whiston, Mr. R. D. Woodall, Mr. H. G. G. Nichols and the Rev. J. E. Noble who also supplied information. In dealing with the prehistory of the district, Mr. Adrian Oswald, F.S.A., Keeper of the Department of Archaeology of the Birmingham Museum, and his staff, especially Mr. P. Gathercole, B.A. (now of the Scunthorpe Museum), were very helpful indeed, particularly in the matter of the Bourne Pool flints ; and I must not forget Mr. Jones of the Bourne Farm, who allowed me to collect the flints from his land. I am grateful to Mr. S. A. Jeavons, F.S.A., for the trouble he has taken to supply the illustrations, and to Mr. A. G. Evans for his help in reading the proofs.

I have made great use of the publications of the Stafford Record Society (previously the William Salt Archaeological Society) ; but for their annual volumes the chapters on the Middle Ages and Tudor times could not have been written.

Dr. J. Stirling, Col. Cartwright and Mr. A. J. Rees have all offered helpful criticism and advice, but they are not in any way responsible for the faults that remain. I am also indebted to the members of the Aldridge Society for their assistance in the publishing of this book, and I must not forget the ready co-operation and advice given by Mr. G. Clark.

The main problem in compiling the history, has been that until recently, Rushall and Pelsall were independent of each other and of Aldridge and Great Barr. As much of what was once Rushall is now in Walsall, and because F. W. Willmore in his *Records of Rushall* has adequately covered most of Rushall history, I have not given the space to Rushall that I have devoted to Aldridge and Great Barr. At Pelsall, apart from the coal-mining era, the population has always been much smaller than that of the other three villages ; and where there are fewer people, usually less history is made. Nevertheless, I believe that much of interest about both Pelsall and Rushall has been included.

At the end of each chapter, I have endeavoured in the Bibliography to summarise the main sources from which I have drawn information. There I have used the following abbreviations :

S.H.C.   The annual volumes of the Stafford Record Society.
B.A.S.T.   Birmingham Archaeological Society Transactions.
B.R.L.   Birmingham Reference Library.
C.R.O.   County Record Office.

If any errors have crept in I apologise for them and would be grateful to be advised of them. Should any reader desire further details of the sources of particular pieces of information, I shall be glad to supply them ; and I would also be pleased to hear of any first-hand information about which I may be ignorant.

The compiling of the book has introduced me to many new friends and given me many hours of pleasure. I hope that this book makes some of that pleasure available to others.

J. T. GOULD.

Aldridge, May 1957

CONTENTS

CHAPTER I

IN THE BEGINNING

HUNDREDS OF MILLIONS OF YEARS AGO, long before any man set foot on soil that was later to become part of the Urban District of Aldridge, forces were at work which were to have great influence on the lives of those who were to live here subsequently. Whoever examines a piece of limestone from Rushall or Hay Head can see embodied in it the fossilised shells of the tiny creatures who lived some three hundred and fifty million years ago. Their bodies have helped to make the thick deposits of limestone which, from Norman times, if not earlier, have provided good building stone for church, manor house, and cottage, besides lime for building and agriculture. Because of these tiny creatures and man's efforts to get the limestone, one road today bears the warning to motorists that it is liable to subsidence; because of them the present canal snakes along from Longwood to Daw End and on to Walsall Wood; because of them part of the district is disfigured with disused limeworks and quarries, though happily the latter are now grassgrown.

Some hundred million years later came the swamps where coal was formed to lie in seams at Pelsall, Leighswood, and Walsall Wood. During the last hundred years many Aldridge men have worked at the dirty and dangerous task of winning that coal ; to them it brought employment ; to some, injury ; and to a few, wealth. To their wives it brought but worry.

Near the coal measures lie the thick beds of Etruria marl from which the famous Staffordshire Blue Bricks are made. Brickmaking has been a local employment since the end of the eighteenth century. Blue bricks from Aldridge have been exported to countries as far distant as Tasmania.

In addition to this natural wealth, high quality ironstone was found at Rushall where in medieval times there were forges, and later, a blast furnace.

The uneven surface of the remainder of the district is made up of sand and bunter gravel. These sandy hills gradually rise to form Barr Beacon, seven hundred feet above sea-level ; some claim that there is no higher land due east of Barr Beacon until the Ural Mountains are reached. This light, sandy, well-drained soil was the most attractive feature of Aldridge for the few prehistoric men who lived here.

Despite the mineral wealth, and the early promise of industry at Rushall, manufactures did not fully develop until the present century ; for transport was difficult and there was an absence of power for the early factories. Before the era of railways and motor lorries, cheap transport of goods meant water transport. Aldridge is as far from the sea and from any navigable river as it is possible for a village in England to be. The local canal was not cut until the end of the eighteenth century. Equally serious was the absence of a powerful stream to work machinery, although it was found possible to use one stream at Rushall to operate the bellows of a small blast-furnace. For centuries geography prevented industrial development, but today the proximity of the over-crowded Black Country, together with the internal combustion engine and electricity make development unavoidable.

CHAPTER II

BEFORE THE NORMANS

HAD THIS HISTORY been written two hundred years earlier, this chapter would probably have been devoted to a lively description of the life and ceremonies of the Druids who were then thought to have lived by Bourne Pool, and to have offered sacrifices and lit their fires on Barr Beacon. Today we are wiser, but since the echoes of the supposed Druids are still heard, it may be as well to dispose of them before dealing with what evidence we have of prehistoric man.

The druid legends first began here in the seventeenth and eighteenth centuries ; there is no mention of them earlier. Some zealous, but rather uncritical antiquarians then leapt on the suggestion of the names "Druid's Heath" and "Barr Beacon", especially as it was then thought that the Druids had their headquarters somewhere in the Midlands ; a belief no longer held. Barr Beacon is not referred to as such in medieval documents, it must be very doubtful that the hill was used as a beacon before the sixteenth century. Medieval documents do however refer to "Druwode" or "Druywode" and to a clearing in Druwode, as when in 1343, Fulk de Bermingham granted Roger de Elyngton (rector of Aldridge) "a certain flat piece of my waste lying in a certain wood called Druywode in the village of Aldridge" (*quondam placeam vasti mei iacentum in quodam bosco vocato Druywode in villa de Alrewych*). Here Druywode means Dru's wood, Dru being the shortened form of the christian name Drogo. We know that a man of that name lived here for in A.D. 1201 he was fined for committing a forest offence, Aldridge then being in the Royal Forest of Cannock. We do not know the nature of his offence, but it might well have been that of cutting down timber in his wood and making the clearing there. With the free spelling of the times, it is an easy step from Druwode to Drewed, the name of one of the open fields of Aldridge, and on to Druid.

In prehistoric times this district, like much of the Midlands, was heavily wooded ; dank oak forest, with a heavy undergrowth of holly and brambles thriving where the soil was heavy. Such land was difficult to clear and was unattractive to early man, especially after he had domesticated animals needing well-drained pasture. The sandy south-east portion of this district was well-drained, and there, possibly, the forest was less dense. The Old Chester Road runs along this sandy portion, and alongside the road are to be found almost all the traces we have of men before Roman times. Most of the traces are just beyond the Urban District boundaries. Starting at Brownhills and working south, is first, Knaves Castle ; a tumulus or burial mound, unexcavated, but believed to be Bronze Age. At Catshill, by the Anchor Bridge, were two more tumuli, but these were partly destroyed and the remains disfigured when the canal was cut there about 1795. Next comes Castle Fort, a small hill-fort, also unexcavated but believed to be Iron Age. On the opposite side of the road is Gainsborough Hill Farm, where the hoard of a Bronze Age smith was found in 1824. The earliest evidence, however, is, strangely enough, where the Druids were believed to have lived, by Bourne Pool. Early antiquarians, Shaw and Hutton especially, described in detail, earthworks by the pool, though these are no longer visible.

On the ploughed surface of an adjacent field, a large number of flint flakes, cores and implements have recently been found. The soil is sandy and well-drained, sloping south to the nearby Bourne Brook. The implements include blades (some of them are very small), scrapers, burins, awls, arrow-tips and one geometric microlith. They are tools suitable for a community of hunters and have affinities with Mesolithic and later cultures. The awls are capable of piercing skins, which may have been worn, whilst the concave scrapers would quickly remove the bark from willow twigs, or smooth the shafts of arrows and javelins. Much of the flint used was of poor quality and was probably collected from glacial drifts ; but some flint was good and was presumably obtained by trading, for there are no deposits of good flint within many miles of Aldridge. At the time of writing, full details of these flints have not been published, but a paper is being prepared by Mr. P. Gathercole, B.A., Curator of the Scunthorpe Museum, and will probably appear in the next volume of Transactions of the Birmingham Archaeological Society (Vol. 74).

Other evidence of early man is to be found at Pelsall and in Sutton Park. On the east bank of the Ford Brook, close to Pelsall station is a grass-grown mound of stones, all broken and cracked by heat, and in Sutton Park, by the Milking Gate, are six similar mounds. These were usually described as "pot-boilers" for it was thought that primitive water vessels could not be exposed to fire, and so water was boiled by dropping in stones that had first been heated. This theory has not been abandoned, but it is now thought that heated stones may have served other purposes also, such as that of drying grain.

Apart from finds of a few scattered flint flakes there is no other evidence of prehistoric man. There is a tumulus (Gossy Knob) close to the Rectory, but this has not been excavated and is probably the mound of an old post windmill ; the round hill in Bourne Vale is believed to be natural and not man-made, whilst the tumulus by Rushall Hall is most likely Saxon, for it is claimed that Saxon coins have been found within it.

During the Roman period the native population was still small and never fully Romanized. The administration would be centred on Wall and Shenstone where Roman goods could be bought and foodstuff, furs, etc., sold. As fragments of Roman glass and tiles have been found at Castle Fort, the British must have continued living there, though there would no longer be the same threat to life and property which led to the immense work of constructing it earlier.

Just outside the Urban District boundary runs the grass-grown Roman road, which is best referred to as Ryknield Street. It runs across Sutton Park, from by the Parson and Clerk, to Little Aston. When first constructed, this road, and the traffic along it, must have greatly impressed the local residents. Soldiers and messengers would pass between Caerleon and York ; there would be merchants from the Continent with wines, Samian and glassware ; whilst to the Continent would pass lead from Flint and Derbyshire, and probably slaves. Roman coins have been found near this road at both Streetly and Little Aston.

Last century it was claimed that an umbo from a Roman shield was found at Hardwick Farm, although this cannot now be found.

A more recent find is a Roman phalera at Great Barr by the Scott Arms. The Romans are said to have quarried limestone at Rushall and Roman coins and a fibula are reputed to have been found there. This claim is not well substantiated and in the absence of other evidence must remain very doubtful. On the other hand, one authority has pronounced that the mortar used by the Romans at Wall included lime made from Wenlock limestone and the nearest supply of limestone in the Wenlock series is at Rushall.

The Saxon conquest of Britain is shrouded in mystery, and in Staffordshire the fog is as impenetrable as anywhere. It was probably during this period that the four villages were first founded as stable communities with entities of their own. In Domesday, Aldridge, Pelsall, and Rushall are referred to by Saxon names. There Aldridge is written as Alrewic—the Alder Village—and if confirmation were needed there is frequent mention of alder groves (alnetum) in medieval documents referring to Aldridge. Pelsall was written Peleshale—the halh or healh of Peol. Presumably Peol was a person but one about whom we know nothing. 'Healh' is a difficult word to translate but is a common element in local place-names. The English Place Name Society give the meaning as including a place that is concealed in some way—an advantage for any village in those troublous times. Rushall or Rischale means the rushy healh.

Great Barr is referred to merely as 'Barra', probably from the Celtic word meaning a summit. This would be in reference to Barr Beacon. It is common for natural features like hills to have retained their Celtic names whilst new villages were given Saxon ones. Another village is also referred to in Domesday as 'Barre' and in order to distinguish between them they were later given the prefixes 'Magna' or 'Great' and 'Parva' or 'Small'. Parva Barr later amalgamated with Perry ('Pirio' in Domesday) to give the present Perry Barr.

Little is known of life in the Saxon villages. The names Wednesbury and Wednesfield (Woden's hill and Woden's field) suggest a nearby centre of Woden worship; but when Mercia became Christian, Chad made Lichfield the religious centre. Aldridge is a mere seven miles from Lichfield so that it is probable that Chad or his followers preached here. Certainly after Chad's death, Aldridge people would flock to his tomb. Bede gives a description of the scene at Lichfield.

Moreover the place of his sepulchre is covered with a wooden tomb made like a little house, having a hole in the side, at which they that come thither for devotions are wont to put their hand and take out some of the dust, the which they put into water and give it to sick beasts or men, whereby the grief of their sickness is, anon, taken away and they restored to their joyful desired health.

With the coming of the Danes and the establishment of the Dane-law would come fighting and insecurity. For a period the nearby Watling Street was the boundary between Saxon and Dane, a boundary too close for comfort and often crossed by raiders. The Viking spearhead, found by a schoolboy—Emlyn Davies—at Great Barr in 1954, bears mute witness to probable events.

Despite the unrest of those times, in A.D. 994 a Saxon lady, Wulfrun, was endowing with land her monastery at Hamtun (hence Wulfrun Hamtun or Wolverhampton). The endowment included land at Pelsall and Ogley Hay. The boundaries were closely defined; those at Pelsall have been translated by W. H. Duignan as follows:

First on Peolsford, along the brook against the stream; thence to the great moor; on the moor, thence on ryehalls to the brook; along the brook against the stream, thence to the hoary (or boundary) willow; from the willow thence on the hart's wallowing place, to the hunters' path, from the hunters' path to Thelford, from Thelford along . . . midstream, thence to Ordsey to the brook, along the brook against the stream, thence to Peolsford again.

Of Wulfrun we know but little, although a lady of that name was captured in A.D. 943 when the Danes sacked Tamworth. In A.D. 997 a charter of King Ethelred was witnessed by one Wulfric who was described as Wulfrun's son.

BIBLIOGRAPHY

S.H.C., Vol. II, p. 104.
Archaeologia, Vol. 21, p. 548.
B.R.L. Scott Charter 608904.
B.A.S.T., Vols. 40, 50, 52, 53, 60.
English Place Name Society, *Chief Elements in English Place Names.*
Fox, *Personality of Britain.*
Domesday Facsimile.
Garner, *Natural History of Staffordshire,* p. 543.
Whitelock, *Anglo Saxon Wills,* p. 152.
Duignan, *Charter of Wulfrun.*
Bede, *Ecclesiastical History,* Book 4, chapter 3.
Willmore, *Records of Rushall.*

CHAPTER III

DOMESDAY AND THE NORMAN FOREST

ALTHOUGH WILLIAM SCORED a resounding victory at Hastings, and thereafter was able to conquer England piecemeal, it was not until three years later that the Midlands were subdued. The leader of Midland resistance was the Herefordshire thane, Edric the Wild, until William routed his forces at Stafford in A.D. 1069. Following that victory William left Staffordshire for York, but returned suddenly before the Saxon forces were regrouped. He proceeded to harry the countryside. We do not know the path his men took, but the entries made in Domesday some seventeen years later are suggestive. There a line of adjacent villages are all described as waste; without inhabitants or cultivated land. The two Hammerwiches, Norton Canes, Wyrley, Ogley, Pelsall and Shelfield are all so described. The Bloxwich entry shows no inhabitants, Bescot also was waste and of Walsall there is no mention (as early as 1446 Domesday was searched in vain for reference to Walsall). Whilst the reduction in population due to the war and subsequent starvation would result in some marginal land falling out of use, it can hardly account for such a string of neighbouring villages; more likely they bear witness to William's policy of teaching the countryside a severe lesson.

Aldridge, Great Barr and Rushall were either more fortunate and escaped destruction, or else recovered more quickly. These three villages with land in eleven counties other than Staffordshire, were given by the Conqueror to William fitz Ansculf, who held the Norman castle at Dudley. He in turn granted them to two knights, no doubt demanding military service and perhaps supplies for his garrison at Dudley in return. Robert (a Norman name) held Aldridge and Great Barr from him, whilst Turchil (a Saxon name) held Rushall. The Domesday entries for Aldridge and Great Barr may be translated as follows:—

Robert holds three hides (units of land) in Aldridge, from William (fitz Ansculf). There is land for three plough(team)s in the demesne (i.e. belonging to Robert) with one slave; and five villeins (farmers) with one cottager have two plough-(team)s. There is one acre of meadow, and woodland pasture five furlongs long and three furlongs wide. It was (i.e. in 1066) and is worth fifteen shillings (per annum). Two free thanes held it and the king had the soc (jurisdiction).

The same man holds three hides in (Great) Barr from William (fitz Ansculf). There is land for three plough(team)s. There is nothing in the demesne, only one villein is there with one cottager. The woodland pasture is a mile long and four furlongs wide. It was and is worth five shillings (per annum). Waga held it.

These two entries hold the key to much subsequent history. Ever since then Great Barr and Aldridge have been linked together and it is impossible to extricate the history of one from the other. Together they formed the manor of Great Barr and Aldridge, with the lord at first residing at Great Barr, but during following centuries seldom living there. The lord of Great Barr and Aldridge soon granted Aldridge as an inferior manor to a family who took as their surname 'de Alrewych', which merely means 'of Aldridge'. This inferior manor was later held by the Hillary, Mountfort, Jordan and Croxall families. The heads of these latter four families seldom resided here. The manor court known as Great Barr and Aldridge dealt almost exclusively with Great Barr matters, for Aldridge had its own court. Matters were further complicated when Aldridge church was built, for then Great Barr was placed in the parish of Aldridge and only became a separate parish during the nineteenth century. When Great Barr residents become restive, as they occasionally do, and ask why they should be linked with Aldridge rather than with Birmingham, West Bromwich or Walsall, they should blame the Conqueror, who gave both villages to William fitz Ansculf, and William fitz Ansculf, who gave both villages to the same lord.

To return to the Domesday record, the entry for Pelsall shows that although it was 'waste' it was still held by the church at Wolverhampton, so that the Conqueror must have respected Wulfrun's endowment. The entry for Rushall can be translated:

Turchil holds one hide in Rushall from William (fitz Ansculf). There is land for two plough(team)s. There is half a plough(team) in the demesne (belonging to

Turchil) and six villeins with two cottagers have a plough(team) and a half. There is a (water)mill worth fourpence (per annum) and an acre of meadow. The woodland pasture is five furlongs long and two furlongs wide. It was (in 1066) and is worth ten shillings (per annum). Wiwara held it with soc and sac (jurisdiction).

Domesday then gives a picture of the four villages, studded in the surrounding waste. At three were small agricultural communities linked to the hated Norman Castle at Dudley. The villeins and cottagers represent heads of families, tied to the soil, farming their own land and that of their lord. The ploughteam consisted of eight oxen or the equivalent in other animals. They would not all be harnessed to the plough simultaneously. Probably four pulled the plough whilst the other four were engaged on the ancillary carting, harrowing, etc. The farmers' wives and daughters would help in the fields, milk the ewes and look after the poultry as well as performing domestic chores and spinning. For the children, were the ox-goad and bird-scaring. Their fare would be augmented by birds and animals from the surrounding waste. Life, however, was far from idyllic; famine being an ever present danger as the Anglo-Saxon Chronicle reminds us. Before long, matters became even more difficult, for when the Royal forest of Cank (Cannock) was created it included Pelsall, Aldridge and Rushall. The southern boundary ran along the Bourne Brook from Weeford to Bourne Vale and the Boltestile (probably the narrow northern ridge of Barr Beacon now represented by Longwood Road), and on to the Holbrook at Walsall. Great Barr was outside the forest but lay within Sutton Chase, held by the Earls of Warwick.

We do not know when this happened but it must have been before 1153 for in that year the Great Register at Lichfield Cathedral refers to Cannock Forest. The forest laws prohibited the hunting of wild animals and placed severe limitations on what the villagers could do with their land. Land already in cultivation could continue to be farmed, but no new land could be enclosed or ploughed, for that would be to destroy the food of the deer; trees could not be felled, for they gave the deer cover; forest courts had to be attended and there were other limitations to prevent poaching. A bow and arrows could not in normal circumstances be carried, and the mastiffs which were kept by the villagers to protect their lockless huts, had to have claws removed from one forepaw. Worst of all, sheep could not be kept without special permission, for they nibbled the grass close and it was thought that their scent was offensive to deer. To a community living near the starvation line this was a dreadful blow, for sheep provided milk (especially for cheese, an essential part of the diet), wool for spinning, and when killed, mutton and skin. The latter could be used for a variety of purposes including that of making parchment. Not until well in the fourteenth century, when the forest laws had been considerably relaxed, is there any mention of sheep or shepherds in this district.

At first the penalties for breaking these laws were savage. Poaching could be punished by mutilation if not death. The penalties were later relaxed in favour of fines (much more profitable to the crown) and imprisonment. The first records we have show that in A.D. 1170 Edward of Barr was fined one mark for an unspecified offence in the forest, whilst in 1176, Robert of Barr was also fined four marks (he paid two and owed two). Previous reference has been made to the offence of Drogo at Aldridge.

The officers who enforced the laws were local men and their offices were often hereditary. Gervase of Bentley was one of these, and when he died (about 1164), William of Rushall claimed the wardship of his heir. Wardship would give custody of the land held by Gervase, and William would also occupy his office. He had to pay five marks for this privilege. He finally cleared this debt in 1166 when he deposited two tallies with the treasury.

The forest official about whom we know most is Nicholas de Alrewych, lord of the manor of Aldridge. Nicholas held the unspectacular offices of Reguarder and Agistor. As one of the Reguarders he had to keep two lists; the first gave details of new offences destroying the food and cover of forest animals; the second gave details of similar offences committed in the past and having permanent effect, the owners of the land being fined every time the Forest Justice visited the district. Sometimes the Justice was not satisfied with the way in which the lists were kept and then the Reguarders were liable for fines as in 1262 and 1271. The Justice only came every seven or eight years; then fines were levied and a record made of them for the treasury officials. In 1271 it was recorded that,

Thomas, son of Matilda of Aldridge has newly occupied an acre in the fee of Felicia of Barr (lady of the manor) and enclosed with ditch and hedge. To be thrown down, fine two shillings.

William de Boweles has enclosed with ditch and hedge half an acre of alders in the fee of Nicholas de Alrewych. To be taken into the King's hands. Fine 'alibi'. Fence to be thrown down.

Alice de Russale for two acres assarted in her own fee. Fine two shillings.

There are many similar entries.

As Agistor, Nicholas had to visit various forest villages and reach agreement with them as to how many animals could be turned out each year to feed on the acorns and beechmast, and how much the village should pay for the privilege. This varied each year. On one occasion Henry III appears to have over-estimated the income, for he ordered that £10 which he had borrowed from Nicholas for Thomas the King's Surgeon should be repaid with ten marks expenses out of this money. The amounts realised during the following years were only as follows :—

1263	£1 17s.	2¼d.
1264	£8 15s.	7¼d.
1265	Nothing through defect of mast.	
1266	£2 6s.	0d.
1267	Nothing through defect of mast.	
1268	£8 9s.	10d.
1269	Nothing through defect of mast.	
1270	Nothing through defect of mast.	
1271	£1 3s.	0d.

Nicholas appears to have been held in very high regard, for his name appears as a witness on numerous charters, and at a time when all the neighbouring lords of the manors were engaged in many lawsuits over property, we have no record (with one possible exception) that Nicholas ever appeared in such a suit as either plaintiff or defendant. Four hundred years after his death, when Erdeswick wrote the first history of Staffordshire, he was able to record that the de Alrewych family were remembered still as being men 'of good repute'. The defaced effigy of Nicholas can still be seen in the chancel of Aldridge church, which he probably founded.

Nicholas was not concerned in the most interesting of forest cases, those of poaching. Indeed, no Aldridge men appear in any of these hearings, although the village was fined in 1262 for not being represented when four men were accused of entering the forest to 'take venison and commit other felonies'. It may be that Aldridge men preferred to cross the Bourne Brook into Sutton Chase and to do their poaching there, for the forest laws did not apply to a private chase. Significantly, in 1346 the Earl of Warwick complained to the King that men were continually entering Sutton Chase and carrying away the Earl's deer. On the list of suspects appears the name of 'William, the parson's bailiff at Aldridge'.

Although as far as we know Aldridge men were not involved, poachers must have often chased their quarry across the nearby waste. The worst case was probably that committed on Christmas Eve, 1263. Ralph Bassett (of Drayton Bassett near Sutton Coldfield) entered the forest with a large retinue and killed some sixteen deer. Ralph was a supporter of Simon de Montfort and was probably at this time gathering followers for the rebellion of the following year. He would need the deer to provide Christmas fare. Eventually Ralph Bassett was killed at the battle of Evesham. Nevertheless the forest officials had recorded the offence, which came before the Forest Justice in 1271. It was reported to him that several of those concerned were then dead, one was in Ireland, two in the Holy Land, and the whereabouts of some of the others was unknown. Only two men were produced before the court, though they may have been held for some years awaiting the visit of the Justice. One of the two was fined twenty shillings and released, the other was 'pardoned for the good of the King's soul and because he is a minstrel'. Frequently offenders absconded and were then outlawed.

An interesting case appears in the Staffordshire Assize Roll 21 Edward I. William Boweles, lord of Rushall, sued the Seneschal of Cannock Forest for taking away the tools and implements of workmen who were working near his house. The Seneschal claimed that the men were working a mine or quarry within the forest without license and so William did not succeed in his action. It seems likely that he was obtaining limestone from the Park Lime Pits, possibly for rebuilding or extending Rushall Hall.

Not only were the forest laws oppressive, but the officers were often dishonest. They did not always have things their own way. In 1288 a mob of some one hundred and ninety men descended on the forest officials at Lichfield, beating, ill-treating and imprisoning them and destroying their records. On another occasion Richard de Bentley was galloping in the forest towards Shelfield, raising a hue and cry after some malefactors. He encountered the Seneschal with his brother and a clerk. These attacked Richard, throwing him from his horse and confiscating his sword, horn, bow and arrows. In this case, as Richard was carrying his weapons on a lawful occasion, he successfully took legal action against the officers.

If the hunting of deer and most other animals was prohibited, hawking was not, save for a short period when that unfortunate king, John, tried to prohibit it. Hugh le Ridere of Aldridge apparently bred his own hawks, for in 1336 he sued John de Oken, chaplain, for breaking into his close at Aldridge, and stealing amongst other things, four eggs of his sparrowhawks worth six shillings and eightpence. The following year Hugh sued another chaplain for stealing five young sparrowhawks worth ten shillings.

BIBLIOGRAPHY

Domesday Facsimile.
Fraser, *Staffordshire Domesday.*
Stenton, *Anglo-Saxon England.*
S.H.C. I, II, V (part 1), VI (part 1).
Richardson, *Medieval Ploughteam* (History, March 1942).
H.M.S.O., Calendar of Patent Rolls, 1346, 1446.
H.M.S.O., Calendar of Liberate Rolls, 1262.

CHAPTER IV

MEDIEVAL LORDS AND PEOPLE

THE EFFIGY OF NICHOLAS is not the only one in Aldridge Church; there lies also the cross-legged figure of Sir Robert de Stapleton, in armour, feet resting on a lion, and carrying his shield with its defiant, fork-tailed, lion rampant; a device well-suited to the man, a grasping, contentious soldier; veteran of many campaigns, lord of the manor of Great Barr and Aldridge, as well as holder of other lands scattered about the Midlands.

Sir Robert was the son of John de Stapleton, who died in 1272 possessed of the manor of Stapleton in Shropshire. In 1282, Sir Robert de Stapleton was at Rhuddlan, ready to proceed with the English army against Llewellyn and the Welsh; he was also fighting the Welsh in 1295, when he was in the retinue of Sir John de Hastinges. He was summoned to Flanders for service in 1297, and for action against Wallace and the Scots in 1301. In this latter campaign many of the English failed to muster, so Sir Robert with two others was sent—

to inquire by jury of the county of Shropshire what bailiffs or ministers have received bribes to stay at home, from the nine hundred footmen selected in the county of Shropshire . . . to attach such persons staying at home and compel them by good manucaption to come without delay to the army at their own expense, and to seize by the sheriff both those who have stayed at home, and those who have taken bribes and keep them in gaol until further order. Also those whom they find to have been guilty hereof, and by the testimony of the sheriff shall appear to have withdrawn themselves, they are to seize by their bodies and goods and to answer to the King for the issues of the latter until such persons come in and promise to submit to justice.

By 1306 he seems to have married the widow of Roger de Ridware and to be lord of Hamstall Ridware, where he was involved in a number of disputes over the ownership of land. In 1310 he witnessed an agreement between Roger de Morteyn and Thomas le

Rous, both of whom were closely connected with Walsall. Meanwhile he had found favour with John de Somery, last Baron of Dudley, who was also a keen soldier. When Sir Robert was in trouble for enclosing forest land, it was Sir John who intervened with the king on his behalf and secured a pardon for him. He was soon in trouble with the king again, for he supported the Earl of Lancaster when the king's favourite, Gaveston, was seized and murdered. He received the king's pardon for this in 1313. In 1317 and 1319 he was again summoned to the army, this time at Newcastle for action against Bruce and the Scots. During a lull in the wars he had taken part in the big tournament held at Dunstable; his arms, a golden lion on a light blue shield, appear in the records of that event (1309). In 1324 he was summoned to attend a Great Council at Westminster.

When John de Somery died, an inquisition was held (1322) into his possessions. It is there recorded that Robert de Stapleton held Great Barr from him. How this happened is a mystery for the manor of Great Barr had passed to Roger de Morteyn by marriage. Roger sold part of his possessions, including his share of the manor of Walsall, to John de Somery, and he may have sold Great Barr to him also, for in 1316 it was certainly in the hands of John de Somery. We do not know how Sir Robert de Stapleton obtained the manor from him, but for many years afterwards, Sir Robert, his widow, Isabel, and her brother, Fulk de Bermingham, were continually engaged in lawsuits with members of the Morteyn family and other members of the Stapleton family, who claimed Great Barr should belong to them. Sir Robert's title must have been very weak, for on three occasions at least, he manufactured false charters (still in existence) showing he had received the manor from different clerks. The production of these charters and the subsequent tracing and summoning of the clerks caused endless delays, meanwhile, of course, Sir Robert still retained Great Barr. Further delays were caused as it was not possible to take legal action against him while he was with the king's army, as he was again in 1332. The following year, 1333, Sir Robert was dead, but we do not know whether he was killed in battle or not. His widow continued to defend the lawsuits with the help of Roger Hillary, eventually Chief Justice of the King's Bench, and who came to include the subordinate manor of Aldridge amongst his many possessions. Isabel was helped by her brother, Fulk, but in 1352 she had to call her steward, William Brown, before the courts to account for his stewardship. In 1370, just before her death, she gave to her then steward, Thomas Jurdan, all his holdings in Aldridge. Four hundred years later, the Jordan family were themselves lords of Aldridge.

Sir Robert de Stapleton was not the only warrior connected with this district. His brother-in-law, Fulk de Bermingham, who eventually succeeded to the manor, was at both Crecy and Calais, as was also William de Boweles of Rushall. William de Boweles' grandson, William Grobbere (or William of Rushall) besides being of the household of Richard II, was with Henry V at Agincourt.

Meanwhile the descendants of Nicholas de Alrewych had been having trouble at Aldridge. About 1277, Nicholas had been succeeded by his son, William, who died leaving a widow, Lettice, and an heir (another William) under age. The wardship of the heir was sold to William Strangelford, who passed it on to Walter Strangelford. William de Alrewych appears to have feared that his guardian might dispose of some of his inheritance, for just before he attained his majority, with the help of many local people, including the rector of Aldridge, Roger Hillary (not to be confused with the Chief Justice), he seized his father's property (1299) together with 'wheat, oats, pigs, capons, hay, apples, and other goods to the value of £40'. Three years later, Walter Strangelford was awarded damages, but the sheriff appears to have had difficulty collecting them and it is doubtful whether Walter was ever paid. This second William de Alrewych died about 1312, leaving yet another William as heir—again under age. This last William entered into his inheritance between 1327 and 1332, but the family fortunes were then at low ebb. No doubt the successive inheritance by two minors was badly felt. William died before 1356 and the manor of Aldridge passed to the Hillary family. The de Alrewych family seem to have left the district following this. One, John, entered the church, another William lived at Lichfield, Richard was in the service of Ralph Bassett in 1378, as was also Nicholas in 1399. In 1401 this Nicholas was with Lady Bassett at Richmond and appears to have gained considerable influence in her service. In 1404 he was sent by the king to bring to London, his enemies who had been captured at Dertemouth 'so the king may communicate with them about the doing, purpose and endeavour of his other enemies beyond the seas'.

When Sir Roger Hillary, the Chief Justice, died in 1356 he held Aldridge from Isabel de Stapleton for the annual rent of three shillings, two barbed arrowheads and a pair of gloves. His residence was at Bescot but he could seldom have been present there, for apart from his duties as Justice, which took him all over England, he was also a member of the Black Prince's Council. He could have given little time to Aldridge, which he probably held only just before his death. He was followed by his son, another Roger, who appeared in many lawsuits, fought with the King's army in France, but appears to have made no impression on Aldridge history.

The Hillarys probably introduced Roger de Elyngton to Aldridge as rector, yet they did not hold the advowson of the church. Roger de Elyngton certainly had close ties with them—he was an executor of the will of the Chief Justice, and it has been claimed that he was originally a clerk in the Court of Common Pleas. He appeared as plaintiff in an action when he sued two men for stealing his horse, worth twenty shillings, other goods worth one hundred shillings and with beating his servant so that he lost his services for a long time. He must have been a man of some substance, for he built the Chapel of the Blessed Peter in Aldridge church and endowed it for a chaplain to say prayers daily for the good of himself, Roger Hillary and others, and for their souls after death.

Meanwhile Rushall was held by the de Boweles family. Sir Hugo de Boweles (a member of Henry III's household) had secured the manor by marriage and was succeeded by his son, grandson and great grandson, all of whom bore the christian name William. The last William died of the Black Death. His widow married William Coleson of Walsall, whilst his daughter married first John Hewet of Walsall and later Robert Grobbere. These families were closely connected with the disastrous events of 1362, when a number of men came

to Walsall armed and arrayed in a warlike manner and besieged the vill by night and by day and had entered the town and broken open the houses of John Flecchere, William Bole, Henry Leverick and many others and had taken divers goods and chattels from them viz. linen and woollen cloths, bows and arrows and other arms to the value of one hundred shillings and had afterwards broken into the smithy of Robert Grubbere and taken divers goods and instruments . . . to the value of £20.

They were also alleged to have killed Richard Colesone, then bailiff of Walsall, John le Grubbere of Walsall, Robert Huwet and John Huwet.

William, the son of Robert Grobbere and the grandson of the last William de Boweles, appears to have been a trusting soul. When he went with the king to France he handed over his property to his friends Hugh de Erdeswick, Thomas Griffin and Richard Horborne, on condition that they should return the property to him when requested. On his return from France they refused to do this, so that William had to petition the Chancellor (John Kemps, Archbishop of York) to assist him as he had no redress at Common Law. His petition appears to have succeeded as his daughter Eleanor and her husband John Harper eventually entered into the property.

John Harper was a man to be reckoned with; he was a Justice of the Peace as well as lord of the manor of Rushall, and secured a great deal of local power. In 1446 he secured letters patent ratifying his right to hold a view of frankpledge twice annually for Rushall and Goscote, together with the right of waifs and strays in Rushall, even if the previous lords of the manor had failed to uphold these privileges. He was concerned in many lawsuits for land and sued many people for debts. Frequently local residents were accused of pasturing cattle on his land, which suggests that he may have made some new enclosures. In 1446 he was excused from serving on assizes, juries, inquisitions, etc., and from holding certain offices. A list was also made of various articles which no buyer or purveyor of the king's household could requisition within his manor. The list gives an insight into the husbandry of those times and includes corn, rye, barley, malt, beans, peas, oats, hay, wood, coals, carts or other carriages, litter, straw, horses, oxen, cows, sheep, calves, swine, fish, rabbits, pheasants, partridges, cocks, hens, capons, chickens, geese or other fowls. Although he was very active as a Justice several of those brought before him escaped because of faulty indictments; though this may indicate bribery in high places rather than incompetence on his part: the Dean of Tamworth had ravished Elizabeth Wright, but escaped because it was not stated in what county the offence had been committed, whilst Richard Hopkys had the outlawry of his father annulled as the process of outlawry did not name the court at which he had been exacted.

If most of what we know of the lords of the manor is based on legal cases, the same is true of the ordinary people. At first they were placed in groups or tithings under a tithing man, the group being responsible for the good behaviour of each member. If one committed an offence the others had to produce him for judgment. In 1185 the tithing of Hubert of Barr was fined one mark because two members had transgressed and the others had failed to produce them; the missing Adam and William had presumably taken to the greenwood. Usually if men fled from justice they were declared to be outlaws and their property was forfeited to the crown. In 1187 the sheriff had to pay six shillings and ninepence and eight shillings and twopence in respect of the property of Richard and Ordricus, both of Barr, who had been outlawed.

Justice could be both swift and crude. In 1272 Matilda of Rowley accused a number of men, including Richard, son of Jordan of Barr, of murdering her husband, Robert. It was found that Robert was a common robber who had killed an accomplice at Walsall and when the accused tried to apprehend him, he defended himself and fled. As he had refused to stand for the king's peace, it was held that the accused had justly killed him.

Apparently witnesses were often dishonest. In 1293 William de Alrewych was a member of a jury investigating whether twenty men were 'common maintainers of false procurers in the King's Court, County and Hundred Courts, taking money from both sides by which truth and justice are stifled'. Half of the accused were found to be guilty.

To serve a powerful lord would give considerable protection. In 1259, when the powerful Roger de Somery proceeded against the insignificant Robert of Pelsall for forcibly abducting one of his villeins from Sedgley, the sheriff returned that he could not find Robert who apparently had taken shelter under the wing of Ralph Bassett at Drayton.

Later the lords put their men in livery; this was illegal, as William de Bermingham found after he had issued green and white cloth to John Hawardyn of Aldridge, carpenter; William Blunhill of Great Barr, yeoman; and John de Gunston of Aldridge, yeoman; but William was eventually pardoned by the king (Henry V).

Powerful men like William de Bermingham caused much unrest

in the district, especially when engaged in a private war of their own, as when Ralph Basset of Drayton was fighting Philip Marmion of Tamworth. Aldridge men on the whole, seem to have avoided being dragged into these quarrels. Some Rushall men were involved though in the case of William de Parles of Handsworth. William was first in trouble when he borrowed £120 from Sampson, son of Sampson, the Jew. As a Jew could not take legal action to recover the debt, Sampson sold the debt to Roger de Somery of Dudley Castle, who seized the manor of Handsworth. Later Geoffrey of Rushall with thirty-eight others was sued by William for cutting wood at Handsworth to the value of £60. Geoffrey and the others produced a deed signed by William which gave them permission to do so. William retorted that at the time the deed was executed he was in the prison of Roger de Somery under duress. Eventually William de Parles was hanged for felony (c. 1271).

There were also eight Rushall men amongst the thirty-four who were accused of besieging Dudley Castle (1329) for two days, shooting arrows and casting stones into it and stealing goods from nearby houses. It was alleged that they were paid threepence per day to insult and besiege the castle.

The violence of the times can be seen from the local murders. In 1293 Richard le Clerk was murdered at Great Barr. Adam Tollet killed the miller of Little Barr in 1299. The Gaol delivery of 1303 shows that William le Fremon of Barr had been killed by men from the Tamworth district. In 1321, 'Andrew de Folleshull, chaplain, conducted two strange men whose names are unknown, in order to kill a strange woman, and they killed her upon the Colefield of Great Barr, recently, by the knowledge and consent of Andrew'. At this time a gang under Roger de Swynnerton were terrorising the district. Amongst many other misdeeds, they stole two pigs from William Cook of Pelsall and pursued Robert de Essington, who was forced to fly to Rushall Hall for refuge, which was then besieged, and arrows were shot over the gate. Eventually a special inquiry was made into the 'illicit assemblies, depredations, burnings and other damages' (1326).

The tax returns show that the population here was still very small. In 1327, Edward III, to meet the expense of the Scottish war, taxed all persons whose movable property, exclusive of armour, jewels, plate and tools, was worth ten shillings. At Aldridge, fifteen men paid £1 8s. 3d.; at Great Barr, Sir Robert de Stapleton and seventeen others paid £2 19s. 9d., and William de Boweles with ten men from Rushall paid £1 10s. od. The Walsall and Wolverhampton figures were £2 11s. 5¼d. and £3 6s. 3d. respectively. Did the large sum from Great Barr reflect the keenness of Sir Robert de Stapleton, for the sums due were assessed locally? More informative is the Poll Tax raised in 1379 by Richard II. This is the tax that helped to spark off Wat Tyler's rebellion. At this time William and Elizabeth Coleson were temporarily holding the manor of Great Barr by virtue of an agreement made with Sir John de Bermingham in 1378. From the returns, the adult population of Great Barr is found to have been as follows:

18 married men (William Coleson, 14 farmers, 2 servants and 1 labourer);

2 widowers (both farmers);

17 other men (1 farmer, 1 labourer, 10 servants and 5 others);

18 married women (the wives of the 18 married men as above);

1 widow;

18 other women (including 14 described as servants).

The term 'servant' appears to have been applied to adult children living with, and presumably serving, their parents.

The list gives no indication of any industry other than agriculture which was on the Open Field system, for charters make reference to 'selions' or strips. A charter of 1327 for example refers to four selions of land in Great Barr lying between the lane leading to the house of Henry the Beadle and the land of Robert the Shepherd. Other charters refer to 'closes' or enclosed fields so that in the fourteenth century both types existed side by side. There were many cases of trespass and of destruction of corn and grass, whilst cattle thieving was not uncommon. In 1423 the Millward of Rushall was accused of killing a calf and twenty sheep, as well as beating the owner. Again in 1436 Thomas Sprotte claimed ten cows and eleven oxen had been stolen from Shelfield, whilst William Hexstalle claimed in 1438 that 12 oxen had been stolen from his close at Great Barr.

The villagers frequently took the law into their own hands. When Thomas Jenkins, in 1473, considered that certain land at Great Barr should belong to him and not to William Frebody, he gathered his friends, broke into the property and, in the words of William Frebody, 'so instilled the fear of death and mutilation in the tenants there, that they gave up their holdings', and he, William, lost their rents.

Drovers were a common cause of complaint, as they walked their animals to and from fairs and markets. The animals would feed on the wayside and commons as they passed. Occasionally the drovers broke into closes as when Thomas Griswold and Richard Constantyne of Solihull broke into the close of Henry Squyer at Great Barr (1432). In this case the drovers are said to have been armed, no doubt to discourage interference by the local inhabitants.

With the open commons, cattle strayed from one village to another, where they would be impounded in the pinfold until a fine was paid for their release, unless the owner illegally 'rescued' them. Such a rescue was effected in 1420 by Thomas Walstewode of Barr, though in this case the cattle had not strayed but had been impounded for non-payment of services and customs due.

There was also much poaching. Roger Stockley sued William Corveser, chaplain, of Walsall, and Thomas Aleyn of Aldridge, for stealing fish from his stew at Aldridge to the value of £20 (1467). On another occasion (1405) William Walsall accused John and Robert Reynolds with William atte Hurst of taking one hundred rabbits from his land at Rushall.

Trees were regarded as a source of wealth and the forest laws against their destruction appear to have been soon relaxed. In 1293 William de Boweles of Rushall sued Henry of Wednesfield for destruction in a wood which he rented. Henry was said to have pulled down a house worth twenty shillings, cut down forty ash trees worth threepence each, and ten pear trees worth twopence each.

Many cases refer to 'barkers'; oak bark may have been used for tanning. In 1451 a consignment of red wine belonging to Humfrey, Duke of Buckingham, passed through Rushall, the carts halting there for the night before continuing the following morning. Thomas Wrasteler of Walsall, equipped himself with a hogshead, and going to the carts after dark, filled the hogshead and took it home. He was accused of this crime and with also having slain (on a different occasion) a man with a handbill. He escaped by producing a pardon from the king. In the different documents referring to his misdeeds, he is called 'Yeoman', 'Barker', and 'Tanner'. Again, in 1431, John Harper sued a Rushall labourer and two Walsall 'barkers' for cutting down eighty of his oak trees and stripping them of bark worth one hundred shillings.

Charcoal burning must have been extensive from the fourteenth century onwards. The 'Colefield' where the burning was done, stretched from the summit of Barr Beacon across to Sutton. It was a lawless district where many crimes were committed. It was sometimes called 'Sutton Colefield' and sometimes the 'Colefield of Great Barr'. It is quite common to find on maps as late as the eighteenth century Barr Beacon and Barr Common marked as 'Sutton Colefield'. Reference has already been made to one of the murders that was committed there, but the case which best shows the size of the industry was when Elias the Collier (i.e., charcoal dealer, for charcoal was usually called 'cole' and what we know as 'coal' was called 'seacole') of London was robbed of £200 on the Colefield of Great Barr in 1320.

Charcoal was needed for the growing metal industries. In the fifteenth century these were developing rapidly and the trade was ceasing to be purely local. William Smyth, 'smith of Great Barr', obtained a pardon (1469) after being outlawed for a debt of £100 due to Hugh Draper of Coventry. Similar pardons were granted to Robert Shellefelle of Walsall for £10 due to Robert Tentyrden of London (1413); Camme of Walsall for one hundred and two shillings due to Thomas Gilmyn of Gloucester (1423, Camme being described as a 'chapman), and Richard Lowe of Walsall 'gentilman or chapman' for forty-seven marks due to John Gryffyth and forty shillings due to Isabella Sutton of London.

Robert Shellefelle or Shelfield appears to have been an ironmonger who travelled the country in search of trade. In 1407 he was proceeding against an innkeeper of Stratford on Avon contending that he had been robbed whilst lodged at his inn. The innkeeper claimed that the door to Robert's room had been fitted with an honest lock and key, but that Robert had admitted some friends to his room when they arrived at the inn later, and that as it must have been his friends who robbed him so Robert had only himself to blame.

The roads locally were so insecure that in 1401 a special commission was sent by the crown to inquire into the report that certain evildoers, scheming to hinder the king's lieges, merchants and others going by roads and highways . . . to the markets of Colleshull, Birmyngham, Walshale, and Duddeley in the counties of Worcester and Warwick, from buying and selling corn, victuals and other necessaries, there assembled in divers conventicles, and veiling their faces with masks, with garments turned in the manner of torturers, and carrying machines called 'gladmeres' and other instruments, lay in ambush and assaulted the king's lieges going to and from the markets and put them and their horses to flight so that the women and children riding on the horses, with sacks filled with corn fell off, and some died, and some were injured, and cut the sacks and scattered the corn along the roads.

BIBLIOGRAPHY

S.H.C., Vols. I, II, III, IV, V, VI, VII, VIII, IX, X, XI, XII, XIII, XIV, XVI, XVIII, XVIII.

New Series III, IV, VI, VII.

1911, 1913.

H.M.S.O., Calendar of Patent Rolls, 1311, 1343, 1401, 1413, 1423, 1429, 1440, 1443, 1446, 1469.

B.R.L. Scott Charters 608893, 608895, 608896.

CHAPTER V

TUDOR TIMES

THE TUDOR PERIOD is often regarded as one of rural depopulation, when arable was turned to pasture, and many who would have worked on the land had to find alternative employment. The generalisation is only partly true for this district. Pasture land certainly increased in proportion to arable, as can be seen from a study of land transfers. By adding the acreage of the different types of land which changed ownership, ignoring transfers where the acreage is not given, or where the bulk of the land was probably not in the four villages, the following figures have been arrived at.

		Area in Acres	
Period	Arable	Meadow	Pasture
Before 1500	290	92	28
1500-1550	610	83	568
1551-1575	1,789	575	1,978
1576-1600	1,202	614	2,368

These figures, taken from chartularies and published extracts of Final Concords, are not fully satisfactory, for the acreage involved in many of the early transfers is not known; land described as waste, furze, wood, heath or moor has been ignored.

The increase in pasture probably represents an increasing use of land previously left waste, especially after 1550, when the population also increased. The Great Barr figures for the Poll Tax of 1379 have already been given, showing a maximum of forty families resident there. A return of 1563 shows thirty-two families then living at Aldridge, fourteen at Pelsall, forty-three at Great Barr and twenty-six at Rushall. The Hearth Tax return of 1666 shows at Aldridge sixty-two households paid, whilst thirty-one were exempt; Pelsall thirty-five paid and fifteen exempt; Great Barr sixty-five paid and fifteen exempt, and at Rushall thirty-nine paid and nine were exempt. The population had doubled, and despite some industry, could only have been supported by bringing more land into use.

A picture of one day in the life of one of the small local farmers is given in the Staffordshire Quarter Session Rolls. Thomas Carm of Walsall Wood was taken before Edward Leigh at Rushall (24th October, 1598) and accused of having stolen a mare. Edward Leigh recorded that Carm

saith that vppon thursdaie was x wickes beinge the xvijth of Auguste he was carringe of his haye halfe yt daye and ij dayes before, and spent the rest of the daye in layinge vp of his haye havinge the helpe of his mother and bodens maied, never going out of his howse till the next morninge nor havinge any bodie in or about his howse to his knowledge but the parties aforesaid all that tyme. He further saith that he never counselled Lyetes boye to tye his mares in any place but duringe the tyme he rought with him, he holpe him to tye them neare his howse where he had corne sowed.

And lykewaies saith that he mowed with Thomas Boden at Aldridge in Branthill feilde till it was about noune (at wch tyme hit rayned and bodens mayed came thether to rake grasse wth whome he went to Aldridge where he bought some bred at Rich. Rocketh and then went whome to his owne howse beinge not past a quarter of an hower past noune, and said that Bodens maied was the first that tould him that Lyetes mare was gone, and his mother at his comminge whome the seconde as he remembreth.

And further saith that he stayed but the eatinge of a little meate at home, and then went to seeke sertaine sheepe that he missed and founde them in the hollyes nere to deepemore beyonde the ground that is now soed in walsall wode on the left hand Lytchfeilde waye about two fleete shoote from Steven Bedders howse, stayed not there but brought his sheepe presentlye awaye nor mett nor se anybodye eyther goinge or comminge but William Geninges wife (wch was reapinge of Barlye) then comminge whome he stayed somme tyme there mowinge grasse in his crofte at home, and then gave over mowinge about fowre or fyve of ye clocke (at wch tyme he went to goodman Lyetes howse) to knowe whether he had harde of his mare or not, And saith that all that tyme of his beinge at home he neyther went to anye bodye or place or had any bodye in his howse that daye or the daye before.

And further saith yt he never shifted him selfe all that daye but ware the same apparell that he put on the morninge wch apparell he vsuallye wrought in all sommer.

Another deposition from a Rushall yeoman shows hawking was still popular. He contended when questioned, that on December 23rd, 1598 he was out hawking from noon until 6 p.m.

Bad harvests still caused food prices to soar, although the Justices at at the Quarter Sessions did their best to prevent this. In 1596, to cheapen corn, maltsters were prohibited from buying barley; ale was not to be sold at less than 2d. per gallon ; and licensed corn-dealers were not to buy corn in the County. Brewing and selling ale was a common device to swell the family income, but in theory all had to apply to the Justices for a license, when sureties for good behaviour were taken, and a promise made that unlawful games like dice, cards, tennis, bowls, quoits, etc., would not be permitted. If the five licensees in Aldridge were not unduly troubled about closing hours they had other difficulties to contend with.

In 16th century documents there is little mention of charcoal burning, but land transfers often refer to furze and heath, which were seldom mentioned earlier. The burning probably had not completely stopped, for in 1591, when Robert Hewes, late of Great Barr, was hanged for an unspecified offence, he was described as a 'collier'. There is still mention too of some trees and woods so that they had not all been destroyed, though the burners had cleared a large stretch of countryside. Much of this open land was common, belonging in theory to the lord of the manor, but with the villagers having rights there, though they had to pay a small fine to the manor court for exercising such rights as temporarily enclosing a portion and cultivating it, or digging turf. Unfortunately, the manor court rolls for the sixteenth century have not survived, but early in the following century there was a dispute between the lords of the manors and details from some of the rolls were entered in a notebook which is now in the William Salt Library at Stafford. The manor of Great Barr and Aldridge included the waste land (Barr Common) on the eastern slope of Barr Beacon stretching north to the open fields of Aldridge; the boundary between the manors was roughly what is now called Knight's Hill and Daniel's Lane. Aldridge men were often in trouble for using this waste, for cutting holly there, digging turf and ploughing. Eventually the Great Barr manor court decided that anyone who did not live at Great Barr, but who ploughed on the waste should be heavily fined—three shillings and fourpence for every day's work, whereas a resident in Great Barr committing the same offence should be fined but sixpence, or if he had first obtained permission, fivepence. It is doubtful if these fees were long exacted for two hundred years later Aldridge men had established definite rights upon Barr Common. The penalty for a similar offence on Drewood Heath in the manor of Aldridge was twopence for a resident and fourpence for non-residents.

The clearing of trees would enable Barr Beacon to be used as a beacon and one may well have been fired there on the approach of the Armada. It is not until well in the next century that the hill is referred to in documents as Barr 'Beacon' but the fact that the Scotts then adopted the beacon as a crest suggests that the use of the hill for this purpose was well established.

Throughout Tudor times there was fear of invasion. In 1539 Henry VIII caused lists to be drawn up of all available men and weapons. The list for Great Barr and Aldridge gives six bowmen without horse or armour, thirty-four footmen armed mainly with bills (poles up to eighteen feet in length, topped with a spearhead and hook, suitable for dragging riders from their horses) and fourteen horsemen with various arms. Of the horsemen, Thomas Chilterne had a bow, Thomas Cooper a steel cap and bill, whilst William Booth had a bill, steel cap with protection for face and neck, a padded leather doublet and protection for the arms. At Pelsall there were but one horseman (with a bill) and four footmen.

William Booth was clearly an important man, but he is one about whom we know very little indeed. He was not lord of the manor, for the manor of Great Barr and Aldridge had passed from the Bermingham family, half going to the Longviles of Wolverton, and half to the Lords Ferrers and on to the Earl of Essex, who in turn sold his rights to William Barrol, who sold them to Robert Stamford of London. The Stamfords came to live at nearby Perry Hall. Nevertheless, the Booths (a Cheshire family) held much land at Great Barr. In 1516 they figured in a case which was heard before the new court—Star Chamber. It involved the ownership of a hundred acre farm at Great Barr. Kateryn Boothe had leased the farm for the duration of her life to Cornysshe and Elyn Cooke, who in turn leased it to Martin Ardern. When Kateryn died, Martin secured a new lease from her heir, Sir William Boothe. After being in possession for seventeen years, Martin was forcibly evicted by Edward Willoughby, who claimed to have bought right to the farm from Cornysshe Cooke. He came to the farm, Heygate, with about twenty-two men, armed with bows, arrows, swords, bucklers and bills. Martin went to law and was reinstated, only for his tenant to be again driven out by Edward Willoughby, who threatened to kill Martin. Consequently Martin appealed to Star Chamber. Edward

Willoughby disputed the terms of the lease from Kateryn, and included an accusation that Cornysshe had secured Kateryn's seal for another purpose and while he had it, made out a lease for the farm to himself, and affixed her seal. Witnesses were produced to dispute this. Some claimed to have remembered the lease-making because afterwards they 'had as good a dinner at Heygate as ever they had'. Apparently it paid to be generous at leasemakings.

The period was also one of religious upheaval. By this time the Presbyterian Leighs were firmly ensconced in Rushall Hall, having married into the Harper family. They no doubt saw to it that the vicars of Rushall were congenial to their views. One vicar, Robert Moore, in his anxiety to make sure that his parishioners did not believe in transubstantiation or worship the sacrament, refused to administer it to them kneeling. As a result, he was summoned before the Quarter Sessions for administering the sacrament 'in form other than appointed in the Book of Common Prayer, contrary to the form of Statute.'

Before this, the chantries as well as the monasteries had been dissolved. During the Middle Ages much land had been given to different churches to maintain a light before the altar, or a priest to pray for the donor's soul. The chantry Roger Elyngton founded is a case in point. These lands were now confiscated by the crown and sold in national blocks. One of these blocks was bought by John Perryent and Thomas Reeve for £3,875 10s. 11¾d. Together with much land in other parts of the kingdom they received,

. . . a close of pasture . . . and a croft . . . in Barre Staffs. which belonged to the late guild of Walsall, Staffs, two closes of pasture . . . in Rushall . . . which belonged to the chantry in Walsall founded by Roger Hillary, Knight; the three cottages and one garden . . . in the parish of Aldriche Staffs. given to anniversaries in the church there; the late chapel of Barre in the said parish of Aldriche, and the walls, stone, timber, glass, iron and roofing and the graveyard of the same . . . a plot or a parcel of moor called Strede Moore (one and a half acres) in tenure of Richard Newman given to a lamp in the said chapel of Barre . . .

The Chapel of Barr had evidently been classed as a chantry and hence the sale. This was soon changed, however, and it came back into use as a Chapel-at-Ease of Aldridge. No doubt the inhabitants grumbled at the confiscations and admitted to no more land belonging to the chantries than they could help. In 1583 the citizens of

Walsall sold to Edward Leigh, land which had been given to maintain an obit in Walsall Church—one wonders how they had managed to retain possession of the land until then.

In 1552, the crown looking further afield, cast covetous eyes on valuable church equipment, and caused an inventory of all church goods to be compiled. At Aldridge was a silver chalice and plate, a copper cross, some vestments, a blue cope, three bells, a sanctus bell, a handbell, two altar cloths and a surplice. At Great Barr was only a little bell, a sanctus bell and a handbell, but a note was added that 'from Barre there was one bell stolne, by whom they know not'. The Rushall list included a chalice of silver with paten, a cope of green silk, two vestments (one of green silk and one of white satin), two crosses of wood (one laid on with brass), a lead cruet, a cloth with a case of red velvet, two brass chanopers, one surplice, two bells and a little bell. At Pelsall were two bells, a silver chalice with paten, some vestments and a cope.

In 1604, John Scott (Rector of Aldridge 1575-1622) was described as being a good lawyer but no preacher, the curate at Pelsall also did not preach, but the Vicar of Rushall, Lawrence Bayley, did. The clergy often farmed their glebes themselves. When Edward Kynnaston, vicar of Rushall, died in 1598 he was possessed of:

One mare	£4	0s.	0d.
One three year old filly ...	£1	13s.	4d.
One cow	£2	0s.	0d.
One pig		3s.	4d.
Eighteen sheep at 4/- each ...	£3	12s.	0d.
Four sheep at 3/- each		12s.	0d.
Corn	£1	8s.	6d.
Hay	£1	4s.	4d.
One saddle and furniture ...		3s.	0d.
One horse lock & pair fetters ...		1s.	0d.
One pack saddle		1s.	4d.
One pitchfork & iron mark ...		1s.	0d.
One 'Troule'?		4s.	0d.
Household Stuff	£2	7s.	6d.
Books	£5	0s.	0d.
Apparel	£7	7s.	4d.
Debts due to him	£55	0s.	0d.

The Quarter Sessions Rolls give intimate glimpses of life here. Francis and Arthur Yoxall were brothers, Francis being the village blacksmith and Arthur the servant of Robert Gorwey of Coppy Hall, who also had a house at Shelfield. One evening Arthur threw a quantity of bedding out of one of the windows of the house at Shelfield, and then hid it in a barn. One Sunday, a little later, he told Francis about this whilst they were travelling together to Wyrley Wake. At that time they tore one of the blankets, thinking that when dyed it would make a jerkin. Arthur also stole from his master a number of cheeses, a quantity of barley and some farm implements which had been left in a field. Francis received most of these goods. They were both tried and found guilty, both pleaded benefit of clergy as they could read, and were duly branded.

Throughout the period the Justices of the Peace had been becoming more and more important. Robert Stamford, of Perry Hall, lord of a moiety of the manor of Great Barr and Aldridge, and Edward Leigh of Rushall Hall, were very active, hearing many cases ranging from theft to disputes over land, and from fixing standard wages within the County to dealing with the upkeep of illegitimate children and the punishment of their parents. Edward Leigh could be very severe on these latter. In 1601 he ordered John Sabin to sit in the stocks at Walsall for three hours on a Sunday afternoon, whilst the mother, Alice Godwin, was to do the same after her churching. In 1599, he ordered a reputed father, Robert Hopkis, to be whipped publicly in the market place at Wolverhampton and to then pay the mother eightpence per week for the next four years. These Justices were not the only local worthies to be hardworked by the crown. Less powerful men like John Jorden and Robert Gorwey of Aldridge, or William Scott of Great Barr, were constantly called on as jurors, while to more humble men fell such posts as constable. The lot of the constable was far from enviable unless he was of powerful physique, especially when he had to deal with people like Edward Stookes of Pelsall. In 1600, six inhabitants of Pelsall were petitioning the Quarter Sessions. They alleged that Edward stole from orchards and that when one owner challenged him, he threw stones at him and 'maimed and hurt him so that he is not able to go without crutches'. Edward was also accused of threatening to kill a servant boy, of fighting with another servant and killing his master's horse with a knife, throwing stones at yet another man, breaking the walls and windows of the house in which he had taken refuge and breaking the boughs of his apple trees. Finally, the petitioners said, he often ran with 'a naked knife, putting people in fear of their lives'.

Meanwhile the industries which were springing up during the Middle Ages continued to grow. At first these were in small metal working smithies like those at Walsall described by Leland. There was not a clear distinction between agriculture and manufacture. When Adam Persehouse (alias Parkes) of Dudley made his will in 1577 he left to his sons, Richard and John, his 'smethies in Aldriche with all implements and woodes', but the other items in his will included 'one cowe and six shepe' to Marie Askew and one heifer each to Eleanor Askew and George Hopkes. Documents of the period refer to George Hollyes of Aldridge, Stirropmaker; John Harrison of Aldridge, salter; Thomas Sutton of Rushall, hiltmaker; Edward Sedgewicke of Barr, nailer; Philip Birde of Great Barr, bucklemaker; and Robert Chamberlayne of Aldridge, wheelwright and alehouse keeper. The trade in lime was also developing for in 1590, Nicholas Pulton of Rushall was fined for selling forty strikes of lime at the lime pit in Rushall, each strike being 'less than the English standard by half'.

Robert Stamford, lord of Great Barr and Aldridge, together with his neighbour and fellow justice, Humfrey Wyrley, were closely connected with industrial development. Together they waged a feud with the Parkes or Persehouses who were rival manufacturers. The course of the feud can be seen from the following details, summarising entries on the Quarter Session Rolls for 1597.

June 15th The Stafford Justices were ordered to return indictments concerning trespasses and contempts by Robert Stamford and others.

July 8th T. Parkes and Richard Parkes of Wednesbury with Ralph Willys and Edward Ashemore of Perry Barr, broke into the furnace mill of R. Stamford and H. Wyrley and expelled William Whorwood who rented it.

July 14th R Stamford, W. Whorwood and about twenty others broke into the mill forge of Thomas Parkes at Handsworth and assaulted his servant there. They also broke into the "furnace for melting and casting iron" at Perry Barr expelling another servant, broke into the house of Richard Tomkys and assaulted Edward Ashemore, whilst at Handsworth they seized the goods of Thomas Parkes which they took away with them on a cart pulled by oxen belonging to

William Whorwood. The goods included 1,000lbs bar iron, 1,500lbs bar iron in 37 pieces, a pair of "chaferie bellows", two pair of "fynerie bellows", seven tongs, three chisels, one great forge hammer etc.

July 16 T. Parkes was expelled from the forge he rented at Wednesbury.

July 18th Supporters of T. Parkes expelled William Whorwood from a smithy he rented at Wednesbury.

July 19th Supporters of Parkes broke into the iron mill of William Whorwood at Perry Barr.

August 13th.   All parties bound over.

So much for the behaviour of the lord of the manor and the local Justices.

A Statute of 1562 prohibited anyone from following an established trade, unless he first served an apprenticeship. Anyone informing of an offender could, for his services, claim half of the resulting fine. Thus in 1594 Edward Ashemore informed against Edward Sudgwicke of Barr, who was carrying on the craft of nailer, and was entitled to half of the fine, £24. Often however the small craftsmen stood together, as when a smith, three nailers and a bucklemaker joined to assault William and Edward Smallwood of Great Barr in 1602; or when John Stone of Walsall, having been arrested by the bailiffs, was rescued by his wife, a servant, three lorimers, two carriers, and a bucklemaker.

Industry continued to grow during the seventeenth century. When Dr. Plot wrote his *Natural History of Staffordshire* he described how lime was made at Rushall. It was quarried by knocking in iron wedges, using great sledgehammers. The stone was then prised up with long levers equipped with rings for the feet of the workmen. The pieces of limestone so obtained weighed up to 150 lbs. each, and often heat was needed to break the stone up. Pits were then made about seven yards long, three yards wide, and two yards in depth. The bottom was lined with wood or gorse and alternate layers of coal and limestone placed on top. The top of the pit was sealed off with a mortar made from slaked lime. In about a week, the gradual burning of the coal reduced the stone to lime.

Dr. Plot also described how iron was made at Rushall. There high-grade ironstone was found in round honeycombed nodules often filled with a liquor 'of a sweet sharp taste, very cold and cuting' but which the workmen drank greedily. The ore was smelted, using charcoal, at the furnace which stood on the land of Henry Leigh. The bellows of the furnace probably were worked by a water wheel.

BIBLIOGRAPHY

Sims, *Calendar of Deeds belonging to Walsall Corporation.*

S.H.C., Quarter Session Rolls, Vols. 1927, 1929, 1930, 1932, 1935, 1940.
Feet of Fines III, IV, XI, XII, XIII, XIV, XV, XVI, XVIII, III N.S., IV N.S., VI N.S., VII N.S., X N.S., 1911.
Also Vols. XVII, IV N.S., X N.S., 1928, 1923, 1915.

H.M.S.O., Calendar of Patent Rolls, 1549, 1550, 1553, 1558.

Midland Record Soc., Vol. 2, *Midland Wills.*

Plot, *Natural History of Staffordshire.*

Wm. Salt Library D634A/30 Notebook.

Caffall, Catalogue of Scott of Great Barr MSS.

CHAPTER VI

THE CIVIL WAR

THE POLITICAL TROUBLES of the Stuarts were not without significance for Aldridge people, though the attempt in 1605 to blow up both Houses of Parliament, together with the king, does not seem to have disturbed the even tenor of village life, save that later it served as an excuse for rejoicing and ringing the church bells, causing the churchwardens to pay special bills to the ringers for their services on November 5th of each year. Powder Plot did cause some trouble to Edward Leigh, who, four days after the event, was busily engaged at Rushall Hall in writing to the Council at London, giving details of the conspirators who had fled to Holbeach House, near Kingswinford. On December 5th of the same year he sent Timothy Hayes, scholar of Douay, to the Council with details of speeches Timothy had made in Walsall about the power of the Pope, as Supreme Head of the Church, to depose the King.

On his coronation, Charles I, like others before him, called on all whose property exceeded a certain value, to come forward and be dubbed knight. A knighthood was an expensive matter, so that many preferred to pay a fine rather than claim the honour. As Charles' real object was to raise money, he was only too pleased that this should be arranged. At Great Barr, William Scott the elder and John Scott senior each paid a fine of £10 to escape. Similar fines were paid by William Scott junior, John Jordan junior, John Jordan senior, all of Aldridge, and Henry Worsey of Rushall, but William Stamford, lord of Great Barr and Aldridge, had to pay £20. These payments bear evidence of the growing importance of the Scott and Jordan families, both having long lived here as small farmers. Now new family fortunes were amassing. In 1629 John Jordan, with John Brandreth of Weeford, was even able to purchase the manor from the Mountfords, and the following year he bought Brandreth's share also. The Scotts had a little longer to wait, but soon after the

Civil War they in turn secured a moiety of the manor of Great Barr.

Meanwhile, Charles I was pursuing his disastrous course, raising taxes as he could and eventually imposing 'Ship Money', which in 1636 amounted to £18 for Barr and Aldridge, and £10 1s. 8d. for Rushall and Goscote, whilst Pelsall escaped with £5 15s. 2d. These sums should be compared with the £32 which Walsall was called on to pay. Tempers were rising and factions were forming. Edward Leigh, eventually Member of Parliament for Stafford (1645) was staunchly Presbyterian and for Parliament. The Stamfords, who had Roman Catholic connections, were for the King, as were most of the other richer families, such as the Holtes of Aston Hall, the Lanes of Bentley and the Hawes of Caldmore. The Jordans and the Scotts appear to have avoided the limelight and the part they played is not clear. Probably most people were indifferent and took the line most appropriate to their own interests when they were obliged to make any decision at all. Such was Richard Pretty, Rector of both Aldridge and Hampton-in-Arden. He was Rector of Aldridge long before the Civil War began; he does not appear to have been active in the Parliamentary cause for on April 30th, 1644, the Committee at Stafford ordered him 'to lend money upon the propositions', which he did accordingly on June 10th of that year; he retained office during Cromwell's time, but as a pluralist he had to relinquish Hampton-in-Arden; he survived the Restoration and was still Rector of Aldridge on his death in 1682. The Registers in Aldridge church only date from 1660, the year of the Restoration. A note at the beginning of the earliest register suggests that the writer had an older register before him at that time, when he probably also copied from the older register the date of burial of two previous rectors. It almost suggests that the old register may have been destroyed deliberately. Was the older register in bad condition? Did the rector object to the entries made during the interregnum by the secular 'Register'? Or was there some other reason?

The first excitement during the Civil War was probably in October, 1642, when Charles with his army passed from Wolverhampton, through Walsall, to Aston, where he stayed with the Holtes. Tradition has it that the next day he reviewed his troops at Kingstanding before passing on through 'malicious Birmingham', where his baggage was looted.

The order of events during the following year is not clear. Most likely Prince Rupert, in April, dealt savagely with the Parliamentarian craftsmen of Birmingham, then passed through Rushall, en route to Lichfield. Edward Leigh had fortified the Hall for Parliament, but was away from home, serving on the County Committee. Prince Rupert attacked the Hall and soon gained it from Mrs. Leigh and the servants, to whom he granted quarter with credit.

Colonel Lane was now installed at the Hall with a garrison of Royalists. From Rushall they raided the Parliamentarian baggage trains as they passed along the Watling Street and Chester Road. In one raid they claimed to have taken nine men at Cannock with sixty horses and fifty-five packs 'wherein were a pretty good store of powder and match'. Significantly, the Stafford Committee (Parliamentarian) recorded on April 15th, 1644, 'that a letter be sent to the chiefe tradesmen in Manchester to forbeare sending any more packs for London until some order be taken for a safe convoy to secure them in theyr journey.'

Later came the siege of Rushall Hall and its capture by the Parliamentarian leader, Earl of Denbigh. This story has often been told (see especially S.H.C. 1910). Briefly, the Earl of Denbigh set out from Stafford on May 25th, 1644, with infantry, horses and cannons (two drakes, two sakers and 'ye Stafford great piece', which was, affectionately known as 'Roaring Meg'). The main body of troops reached Bloxwich and remained there that night, Saturday, though some horse moved on and surrounded Rushall Hall. Sunday was spent at Walsall, but some infantry moved up to the Hall where an alarm was caused by a woman attempting to escape from the Hall to fetch help from Lichfield. On Monday a start was made to get the artillery into position for the attack, but the besieged managed to wound the officer supervising this so that the cannons were not in position until the following morning. The Parliamentarian forces needed food and supplies, so parties were sent out to scour the neighbourhood. As both sides probably took a periodical levy for the forces in the neighbourhood, this new demand was not welcome and threats had to be used. Meanwhile, scaling ladders and other apparatus were assembled for an assault on Tuesday. Tuesday, however, saw fresh delays for there was news of a large Royalist force approaching Lichfield. A scouting force was sent out, and had a brush with the enemy, who made no attempt to come to Rushall. On Wednesday morning, the artillery opened fire on the Hall, and at nine a.m. there was a lull whilst the attackers called on the besieged to surrender. This was confidently refused and the firing was resumed until four p.m., by which time a large breach had been made in the walls. The defenders had also garrisoned the nearby church and peppered the attackers from the tower, until a cannon was trained on the steeple and part of the battlements shot down. The Earl of Denbigh called a council of war and it was decided to storm the Hall at night, but before then, the besieged asked for a parley. Denbigh stated his terms for surrender, which were refused, but on receiving from his officers, who had entered the Hall, a report on the strength of the defences, he modified his terms, which were then accepted. The garrison then marched out unarmed, and were given safe conduct to Lichfield, where Colonel Lane is reputed to have been ill-received by his cousin, Colonel Harvey Baggott, who deplored the surrender. When the Parliamentarians entered the Hall, they found there, in addition to gunpowder and provisions, one drake, one hundred muskets, twenty fowling pieces, six pair of pistols, one hundred and thirteen rolls of tobacco and one barrel of cut tobacco. A Captain Tuthill was installed as Governor and given power to exact a levy for the maintenance of his forces from Aldridge, Barr, Rushall, Walsall, Handsworth, Tipton, Willenhall and other communities in the neighbourhood. The weekly levy from these places was found to be insufficient, so that on March 10th, 1645, Captain Tuthill was given permission by the Stafford Committee to collect a special levy of £90 from eight named persons who probably had not actively supported the Parliamentarians, or perhaps they were recusants. They included John Harrison of Aldridge £6, Thomas Harrison of Aldridge £4, John Adcock of Nether Stonnall £10, and Humfrey Wyrley of Hamsted £20. When Sanders wrote his history of Shenstone he was able to record that the following receipt had been issued:

Forasmuch as John Adcock, of Nether Stonnall, hath advanced upon the proposition of Parliament the sum of £8 and hath paid the same into the receipt of this garrison of Rushall howse. Theis are therefore to command and charge all officers and soldiers under my command and request all other forces for king and parliament, not to molest, vex, trouble, or offer any violence to the said John Adcock, nor to plunder, pillage or meddle with any of his goods or chattels, he, the said John still continuing a friend to king and parliament, and not doing or consenting to the doinge anything prejudicial to the kingdom and state. Given under my hand at the garrison of Rushall howse for king and parliament this 9 day of May 1645. Robert Tuthill.

Despite the fact that they were fighting against the king, the Parliamentarians always described their party as being for 'king and parliament'. One account book shows that Parliamentarian forces received a total of £272 10s. 11d. from Barr and Aldridge, £117 0s. 0d. from Rushall and Goscote, and £130 19s. 3d. from Pelsall.

The Royalists were not content to allow Captain Tuthill to remain at Rushall, where he was probably as big a nuisance to them as Colonel Lane had been to their enemies. Rushall was sufficiently near the Royalist garrisons of Lichfield and Dudley to have considerable nuisance value. By 1644 things were going badly for the king and probably the local garrisons were not strong enough to make a direct assault on Rushall; instead they resorted to bribery. Francis Pitt (sometimes referred to as Thomas Pits) was a Wednesfield farmer, aged sixty-five. He was known to the garrison at Rushall Hall, having called there several times to pay the levy. His landlord was Colonel Leveson, who was now the Royalist commander at Dudley. Leveson offered Pitt free tenancy for seven years if he would help secure the surrender of Rushall Hall. By means of Pitt, Captain Tuthill was offered £2,000 to surrender. He appeared to accept and promised Pitt £100 of it for his services. He insisted that Leveson should first release some prisoners that he held. At eleven p.m. on September 9th Colonel Leveson rode out of Dudley with eighty men to take over Rushall Hall. On arrival there, they gave the password, but instead of the gates being opened for them, they were greeted with a volley from the waiting garrison. Captain Tuthill had played them false. Pitt was captured and sent to London for trial and being found guilty was hanged from a gibbet in Smithfield. Tuthill also had to give a full account of the affair, apparently his own party mistrusted the part he had played, but he succeeded in satisfying them of his loyalty. Before he died, Pitt described the garrison at Rushall Hall, and his description was included in a Roundhead pamphlet:

Now concerning my being in Garrison in Russell-Hall in Staffordshire, being urged by Master Smart, Minister of Gods Word, to deliver my opinion concerning them. For their profession, they do all professe God; but I never heard nor saw, so much swearing or drunkenesse, and other prophanations, as was in that place: For the Martiall of that place, he would swear and domineer, and was so discontented, as if he would cause the stones to flie out of the Walls.

Presumably, the Marshall referred to was Captain Tuthill.

Meanwhile, Edward Stamford, lord of Great Barr and Aldridge, fought on the king's side and as a result his estates were 'sequestrated'. His wife pleaded with the Stafford Committee that she was destitute, so the Committee agreed that she should remain at Perry Hall and should be allowed to receive one-fifth of the income from the estate, provided that she, like everyone else, made the weekly contribution for the maintenance of Parliamentarian troops in the county. The estate was administered on behalf of the Committee and Mrs. Stamford, by Mr. Erpe of Stonnall and Mr. Thomas Jorden of Perry Barr. Mrs. Stamford agreed to prevent any molestation of Mr. Erpe by the Royalists whilst the Committee were to protect Mr. Jorden from the Parliamentarian troops. Meanwhile, 'Lieutenant Colonell' Stamford, who had been captured by the Roundheads in 1644, was confined in Eccleshall Castle.

The end of the Civil War brought more troubles for Sir Edward Leigh. He personally was against the execution of the King, and so at the time of Pride's Purge, he was excluded from Parliament, to which he had been elected in 1645 as Member for Stafford, when the previously elected Royalist Members were disabled. He was temporarily imprisoned at the King's Head in the Strand, but was soon released, and in March, 1649 was sent to Munster as one of the three Commissioners. He returned to Parliament in March, 1660 but retired from public life at the Restoration. Besides being a Member of Parliament, presbyterian, soldier and rebel, he was also theologian and author. His best known book was *Critica Sacra*, which was a standard reference book for many years. His most disappointing book, at least to the local historian, is his *England Described*, which adds nothing to our knowledge of this area, being merely a re-hash of what others had written earlier. The best remembered incident in his colourful career was trivial. In 1629 he played a game of bowls at Bloxwich before a crowd of onlookers.

By a law made during Henry VIII's reign, bowls was an unlawful game and the mayor of Walsall had him seized and imprisoned. His counter-action against the mayor for unlawful imprisonment was dismissed, the mayor being Mr. Henry Stone. As member of the Stafford Committee, Edward Leigh had as fellow committee man Captain Henry Stone of Walsall, and when a dispute over the Earl of Denbigh divided the Committee into two factions, it is not surprising to find they took opposite sides. (More detailed summaries of Edward Leigh's career are to be found in S.H.C. 1920 and in the recently published history of Queen Mary's Grammar School, Walsall.)

BIBLIOGRAPHY

S.H.C., Vols. II, 1910, 1931, I (fourth series).

The Confession of Thomas Pits (pamphlet, 1644).

A More Exact and Perfect Relation of the Treachery, Apprehension, Conviction, Condemnation, Confession and Execution of Francis Pitt. (Pamphlet, 1644, reprinted 1881 by W. H. Robinson, Walsall.)

Sanders, *History of Shenstone.*

Willmore, *Records of Rushall.*

Guttery, *The Great Civil War in the Midland Parishes.*

Sims, *Calendar of Deeds and Documents belonging to the Corporation of Walsall.*

CHAPTER VII

THE FARMERS

FARMING IN THE MIDDLE AGES at Great Barr, Rushall and Aldridge was in the Open Fields, with the different farmers owning scattered strips. These were supplemented by many small enclosures from the surrounding waste. The Open Fields also would be extended as the population grew. After the Tudor period, documents cease referring to strips at Great Barr and Rushall, so it is probable that the Open Fields there were enclosed during the sixteenth century, the strips giving way to the type of field or close with which we are familiar today.

At Aldridge the unenclosed strips persisted until well into the eighteenth century. A terrier of 1684 gives details of ninety-six of these strips which belonged to the church. Of these, forty-four strips were in Drewed Field, twenty-seven in Brantial Field, seventeen in Daniel Field, and eight in Wetstone Field. The strips in Wetstone Field were all in one block, as were also twenty-eight of those in Drewed Field. The rest were mainly in scattered single and double strips. Drewed Field roughly occupied the land between Hobs Hole Lane and the present Little Aston Road (then known as Field Lane). The position of the other three fields is still indicated by Branton Hill Lane, Daniel Lane and Whetstone Lane. Middlemore was another Open Field, but probably much smaller. Westbroc Field and Paddock Field may or may not have been open.

In 1758 another terrier was compiled. This time there is no mention of strips; instead, the land is described as being in ten different 'flatts' or fields. Typical is 'Taken out of Branthill Field, four flatts, one containing four acres, Mr. Jordan, east; Mr. Cox of Walsall, west; Mr. Jordan, north and Mr. Penn, south . . .' The fields had been enclosed and redistributed. It is infuriating to find no details how this was accomplished for there must have been a major upheaval. No Act of Parliament was secured and one can only assume that it was achieved by common consent in the manor court.

With Open Fields, a manor court was essential: there, under the lord's steward, decisions were taken about the crops to be sown, the dates to commence ploughing and sowing, how the animals were to be kept off the crops and so on. Transfers of land were also recorded and fines levied for not cleaning ditches, encroachments, etc. The court also administered the commons. Four rolls have survived for the Great Barr court and two for the Aldridge court. All the Great Barr rolls refer to the period after the Open Fields had been enclosed.

The earliest roll for Great Barr is dated 1610. There were then two lords of the manor who apparently divided the land up, so that Sir Henry Longvile of Wolverton was regarded as lord of some land, and Edward Stamford of Perry Hall, lord of the rest. The two lords, however, had a joint steward and held a joint court. The roll begins by excusing Thomas Cox, Richard Cox, Thomas Jorden senior, John Wilcox, and Thomas Bromwich from attendance. Then follows a list of twelve jurymen and the names of twenty-six land-holders who were absent. These latter were fined sums ranging from fourpence to sixpence. William Freeman had died and his son, to enter into his inheritance, had to pay a fine (heriot) of half the annual rent (four shillings and threepence) to Edward Stamford. A number of transfers of land were also recorded from Sir Edward Leigh to Thomas Jorden, William Jorden, William Scott, John Scott and Edward Harryson, whilst John Scott had sold his farm 'Veysies' (Pheasey) to William Scott. A number of Aldridge men who had been ploughing on the Colefield (Barr Common) were fined amounts ranging from ten shillings to thirty-nine shillings. Sir Edward Mountford, lord of Aldridge, was fined ten shillings on account of Bourne Pool, and Richard Parke, also, ten shillings for not moving his timber off the lords' waste. He was ordered to rectify matters before next Pentecost and to fill up any holes made. John Bridle and Roger Turton had to pay for not cleaning their ditches (three shillings and fourpence and ten shillings respectively). William Jorden, Thomas Daye, and Laurence Gibson had cut turf from the common, it cost them sixpence each; whilst Thomas Addyes, who had edged his boundary forward on to the common, was fined one shilling and ordered to rectify matters. The last entry on the roll is not clear but appears to impose a fine on three men for an offence concerning rabbits on the common. The rabbits were reputed to have been very numerous and after the manor court had lost most of its power entries appear in the accounts of the parish constable, such as

1773. 14 Nov. Expenses on Thomas Garrett and takeing him to Bridewell for catching rabbits . . . 16s. od.

The second Great Barr roll (1612) is similar but the fines are much smaller, fourpence for encroachment, one shilling for ploughing on the common and twopence for digging turf. The last two entries, partly disfigured, are interesting. The first seems to rule that land enclosed from the common with permission, could be cultivated for four years after which, it had to return to the common and be allowed at least seven years to recover before it could be again enclosed. The second entry imposed a fine of five shillings on Edward Weston for taking a cartload of sand out of Hemcross Lane. He was fined, not for destroying the road, but for taking the lord's sand without permission.

The other two Great Barr rolls (1685 and 1725) also follow the same pattern, but attached to the latter roll was a list of thirty-one encroachments (this list is now catalogued as a separate item in the Birmingham Reference Library). The encroachments show how Great Barr was developing, for no fewer than ten of the items refer to land taken from the common for a cottage. John Hoo was lord of the manor, residing at the Old Hall in Great Barr. As the fine imposed for these cottages was only fourpence each it can be assumed that he was favourably disposed towards the squatters. Most of the other twenty-one encroachments refer to land added to existing cottages, one is for a well to be built, another is for a carthouse, whilst one reads 'the sheep washers for ye sheep penn'.

The 1685 roll terminates with four rules concerning the use of the commons. They may be summarised as follows:

1. Rams not to be allowed loose on the common after September 15th in any year. Fine three shillings and fourpence.
2. Peat or turf not to be cut before May 8th in any year. In no case is turf to be given or sold to those who do not reside in the manor.

3. People enclosing land on the common and sowing it with corn, must help fence the animals off. Fine for every gap, one shilling; and for every perch three shillings and fourpence.
4. No one to cut or burn fern on the common before June 24th, and no one to cut gorse growing on any ditch or bank.

The cutting of turf was a common practice in Staffordshire. Dr. Plot in his history refers to the uses to which the turf was put at the time he was writing (1686). He says:

. . . the turf which they cut in the Moorelands in the Springtime with an instrument called a push-plough, being a sort of spade, shod somewhat in the form of an arrow with a wing at one side and having a cross piece of wood, and the upper end of the helve after the manner of a crutch, to which they often fasten a pillow, which setting to their thigh and so thrusting it forward, they will commonly dispatch a large turf at two cuts, and then turn it up to dry, which in good weather is done on one side in eight, and on the other in four or five days at the most: when dried if they intend them for fuel in the winter, they pile them up round in the manner of a hayrick ten or twelve feet high, and let them stand all summer. But if for manuring their land, they heap it up . . . and set it on fire which will take of itself if it be dry, otherwise they give it the assistance of wood. These heaps they will keep burning sometimes three weeks together, still covering them over with new turf as the old ones burn away, only giving them vent by airholes which they make with a stick. The ashes of these turves they call Ess, which laid on their meddows, rye or barley lands, some are of the opinion goes further than lime or dung. And these are all the uses they put their turf to . . . only they use it frequently to ridge or head their meaner houses, and sometimes wholly thatch them with it.

Dr. Plot also refers to the then current practice of burning fern, in June:

. . . when green which . . . they most commonly doe it on the side of a hill . . . lying to a fresh gale of wind. I was told that they burnt it green that the ashes might not fly away during the operation . . . but I guess the true reason may rather be that while it is green it hath an oilyness which doth not quite consume, but remaining mixed with the ashes, makes them fitter to the use they are ordinarily put to, these made up into balls about three inches in diameter by the poorer sort of people with warm water, being sold at five or six a penny to wash their buckings (linen, etc.) with the year about.

Other contemporary writers such as Celia Fiennes also refer to this practice. Judicious firing of the commons may have also improved the land for sheep grazing, but it would be most unpopular with sportsmen, spoiling both hunting and shooting. In 1769, John Hoo inserted an advertisement in *Aris's Birmingham Gazette* offering a reward of no less than five guineas (a labourer then earned about ten shillings per week) for information leading to the conviction of men who had started a fire on Barr Common. The following entry also appears in the parish constable's accounts for April 30th, 1758:

Charges about two men for firing ye ling on ye common
  Spent in eating and drink ....5s. 0d.
  Taking them to Mr. Whyrley and Wolverhampton   3s. 0d.

Mr. Whyrley would be a Justice of the Peace.

The fourth rule on the court roll also refers to the cutting of gorse. This would be used for firing, and also (according to Plot) to form the base of cornstacks, mice being unable to climb through the gorse and into the stack.

The first Court Roll for Aldridge (1714) is headed 'Manor of Offlow' but is the record of the Court Leet and Court Baron of Thomas Jordan (the Jordans had bought the Court Leet and the Manor from the Mountfords in 1629, but in 1720 they sold the Court Leet to Edward, Lord Leigh, whilst retaining the manor). The roll shows the court as meeting at 'ye sign of ye Anchor' and proceeds to lay down the following rules:

1. All fences round Aldridge winter corn fields to be repaired within fifteen days of the first sowing and to be maintained until the 'corne be Inned'. Fine 3/4 per perch and 5/- per gap.

2. All fences about Aldridge Lent corn fields to be repaired by March 24th and to be maintained until the harvest. Fine 3/4 per perch and 5/- per gap.

3. All persons having sheep upon the Commons to take out the 'Rudgells' and to keep them off the Common from St. Bartholomew's Day until Christmas.

4. Mares and foals not to be tethered on the Common fields after the foal is ten days old. Fine 50/-.

5. All swine to be 'rung' upon three days' notice. Fine 3/4.

6. No gorse or heath to be cut on the ditchbanks. Fine 50/-.

7. No servant to keep more than six sheep on the commons. Fine £10.

The roll closes with Court Leet business nominating Paul Griffis, Constable of Great Barr and Thomas Davies, Thirdborough.

The second court roll for Aldridge (1770) shows the court as again meeting at 'the sign of ye Anchor and King's Arms', under the steward of Edward Croxall of Shustoke, who was then lord of the manor. Apparently this was the first court held since 1766, and the court proceeded to order that enclosures on the common authorised at the last court, should now be thrown open or a fine of thirty-nine shillings exacted. It was ordered that no person claiming right of commons should turn out more cattle on the common than their lands 'can be reasonably supposed to support and maintain', fine thirty-five shillings for each offence. It must be very doubtful if this rather vague rule was enforced. At Aldridge there were many small landowners and the practice earlier seems to have been 'right of common without stint'.

Farmers have always grumbled about the payment of tithes and the Aldridge farmers were no exception. During the eighteenth century the Aldridge rector seems to have exacted his tithes in kind, for a terrier of 1773 ends with:

All tythes are due to the Rector, both Small and Great such as Corn and Hay, Calves, Lambs, Piggs and Geese etc. and everything Except a modus of one part of Great Barr for grass etc.

Great Barr, of course, was then still in Aldridge parish. By 1823 the tithes had been commuted to money payments, and a return of 1833 shows 2,145 acres of arable and 570 acres of meadow and pasture yielding tithes amounting to no less than £1,098 per annum. No wonder the farmers grumbled. A labourer at that time earned about ten shillings per week.

In 1795 a movement was commenced to enclose the commons of Great Barr. Mrs. Eliza Foley and Mrs. Whitby were then the ladies of the manor. On January 14th a petition was presented to the House of Commons in their names and those of the Hon. Edward Foley and other landowners claiming Barr Beacon and other wasteland within the manor to the extent of 2,200 acres,

in their present state afford very little advantage to the several persons interested therein, but if the same were inclosed and divided up into specific allotments to the several persons interested a very considerable benefit would arise from the Improvement and Cultivation thereof.

Leave was granted for a Private Bill for dividing and allotting the commons to be prepared and presented. A contemporary description of Barr Common appeared soon afterwards in Pitt's *Agriculture of Staffordshire*. It described how there grazed large flocks of grey-faced sheep, similar to those of Cannock Chase only bigger. That part of the Common which was in Staffordshire (i.e., the Great Barr and Little Aston portion) was said to support 11,000 sheep in summer, and that more could have been supported if the number of rabbits had been reduced. The district was 'a barren sheep walk containing in some large tracts scarcely any other plant than heath, in other places fern, gorse, whortleberries and rushes with grass in small proportion'. Pitt estimated it to be worth three shillings and sixpence per acre, but if enclosed ten shillings and sixpence per acre.

On January 21st, Sir Edward Littleton, M.P. for Staffordshire, introduced the bill, which was received and read the first time. The second reading followed on January 26th, when the bill was committed to Sir Edward Littleton and the Earl of Sutherland, who were to meet as a Committee in the Speaker's chamber at five p.m. that evening, to consider the Bill and any objections raised. Sir Edward Littleton reported to the House on February 3rd that the Bill had been examined and was found to be in order and that the parties concerned (i.e., the landowners) had all given their assent except one person whose property was rated for Land Tax at three shillings and who opposed the enclosure, and one other person whose property was rated at eightpence who would not declare for or against the Bill. The Committee had made some amendments but no one had appeared to oppose the Bill. The amendments were accepted and the Bill received a third reading the following day when Sir Edward Littleton then carried it to the House of Lords, who agreed to the Bill and returned it on February 12th. It received the Royal Assent the next day. The whole process took less than a calendar month. An examination of the Land Tax returns shows that the gentleman who would not agree to the Bill must have been William Dilke, Esq., a wealthy landowner who did not reside in the manor. The man who would not declare for or against the Bill must have been Matthew Glover, a resident, but one owning very little land. His attitude is hard to understand unless he wished to oppose the Bill but was frightened of the possible results of downright opposition to his more influential neighbours. The tenants, who exercised the rights of common vested in the property they rented, and who used the common for turf, firing, etc., were not consulted. They have left no indication of their feelings, but if they had wished to oppose the Bill it is doubtful if they could have afforded to do so, and in any case the speed with which the Bill was passed left them very little opportunity. On March 22nd a notice appeared on the doors of Great Barr Chapel and Aldridge Church informing the parishioners that the enclosures were to be made and that the Commissioners would hold their first meeting on April 6th at the house of William Wight, Innkeeper.

The lord of the manor of Aldridge (Edward Croxall of Shustoke) and the Aldridge landowners (who claimed to have rights on Barr Common) could have opposed the Bill. Perhaps they did in the early stages, for the Bill in its final form made a full recognition of their rights, and allowed them a share of Barr Common. Thereafter Aldridge landowners were mainly concerned with getting the Aldridge commons also enclosed with a minimum of delay. In all there were 360 acres of common. One difficulty was soon experienced. The lord of the manor was sure of a share in the enclosure in return for his 'manorial rights', quite irrespective of any land he may have owned directly. William Smallwood came forward and disputed the claim of Edward Croxall to the manor. He produced a document showing that the manor had been sold some years earlier and that by right he was lord of the manor. Edward Croxall naturally refuted this and the matter went to the Quarter Sessions where Croxall's claim to the manor was easily upheld. This dispute took time, but rather than delay the application for permission to enclose the commons, Parliament was petitioned for leave to prepare and introduce the necessary Bill. On February 4th, 1795, the petition bearing the names of 'Edward Croxall Esquire, and William Smallwood, gentleman, claimants of the Manor and soil within the Township of Aldridge' and that of the Rector and other landowners was presented. Leave was duly given to Sir Edward Littleton and Mr. Wilberforce (the leader of the anti-slavery movement) to prepare and bring in a Bill. It passed through the same procedure as the Great Barr Bill but took a little longer. It received the Royal Assent on June 22nd. When the landowners of Aldridge had been approached there had been some opposition, for at Aldridge were many small proprietors. Owners of land assessed at twelve shillings and a halfpenny opposed the Bill, whilst owners of property valued at two pounds and elevenpence declared themselves neutral. Again no one opposed to the enclosures appeared before the Committee. Sir Edward Littleton, who did so much to promote both Bills, said a few years later when speaking of his own estate and referring to labourers' cottages:

. . . if by the side of a common the better, as furze will supply the oven with fuel, and a few sheep or geese may be kept. Every labourer should have keep for one cow. . . .

No provision was made for the labourers at Great Barr or Aldridge, although the Court Roll cited above (1714) admitted the right of servants to pasture six sheep on the Common.

Even after an Enclosure Act had been passed the work of enclosing the Commons was a lengthy process. Claims for a share had to be considered, the land surveyed, valued, and allocated, and a map drawn. The awards were not completed until June, 1799. At Great Barr, the ladies of the manor were allowed one sixteenth share of the Commons in lieu of their manorial rights; this allotment was to be entred on the clump of trees then standing on the crest of Barr Beacon. The ladies were also allowed six months to remove any wood they desired from the Common. In all, 1,989 acres were enclosed, as follows:

Provision for roads	68 acres
The ladies of the manor, and their heirs, the Scotts	943 acres
Lord of Aldridge	137 acres
Seventy-three proprietors of land in Aldridge	475 acres
Thirty-nine proprietors of land at Great Barr	366 acres

The allotments to the ladies of the manor, the Scotts and the Lord of Aldridge were not merely for manorial rights but included their shares as extensive landowners. Of the allotments made, thirty-one claimants received less than one acre and forty-seven between one and five acres. Those receiving land were to complete the enclosures with ditches, quickset hedges and proper mounds before April 5th, 1800. Failure to complete enclosure meant a neighbour could do the fencing and reclaim the cost through a local J.P., who could levy distress on the defaulter's goods. In addition, recipients had to share the cost of making the roads, promoting the Bill, surveying, valuing, etc. No wonder nineteen claimants had sold their rights to allotments before the award had even been completed.

At Aldridge only 344 acres were enclosed, and this was divided between seventy-eight claimants. The allotment for manorial rights was twenty-one acres, but Edward Croxall also received seventy-two acres for the property he owned. The Rector received five and a half acres for his Glebe and was excused all costs of fencing, etc. Twenty-seven people received less than one acre. Finally, all proprietors were to pay their share of the costs of promoting the act, etc., to the solicitor (the son of the lord of the manor) within thirty days of the award being made.

The new proprietors were soon asserting their rights. In the Poor Law Accounts of Aldridge appears the following note dated April 15th, 1799:

It was also ordered and agreed from and after May 1st next, all cattle and sheep found upon the new inclosures within the said parish shall be impounded by a person appointed at the said meeting, and the damages to be received by him shall be as follows

For sheep & lambs per head...1d.

For asses, cows and horned cattle...6d.

For horses ....1s. od.

For pigs 6d

The above charges to be made to parishioners and double the same to be made to extra-parishioners. It was further ordered that Thomas Needham be appointed to impound as aforesaid and that he be paid ten shillings per week for his trouble deducting all money received by him according to the rates above mentioned.

In the Great Barr Poor Law Accounts appears:

1800 Nov. 7th   John Boden for impounding sheep etc. £4 3s. 6d.

1801 Nov. 6th   John Boden for impounding sheep etc. £4 17s. od.

BIBLIOGRAPHY

C.R.O., Aldridge Poor Law Accounts.
            Aldridge Terriers 1684, 1758, 1773.
            Aldridge Manor Court Roll, 1770.
            Great Barr Manor Court Roll, 1610.
            Great Barr Enclosure Award.
            Aldridge Enclosure Award.
            Land Tax Returns.
B.R.L., Great Barr Manor Court Rolls, 1612, 1685, 1712, Offlow 1714. (359706).
Parish Chest, Gt. Barr Constables' Accounts.
                    Poor Law Accounts.
Plot, *Natural History of Staffordshire.*
Pitt, *Agriculture of Staffordshire*, 2nd Edtn., 1808.
House of Commons Journal, 1795.

CHAPTER VIII

THE RICH AND THE POOR

EARLY IN THE EIGHTEENTH CENTURY, John Hoo was lord of the manor of Great Barr. The manor court roll referred to in the previous chapter suggests that he was a lenient lord and this is supported by the few odd details that can still be discovered about him. The record of briefs in Bilston Chapel reveals that when William Page of Great Barr suffered considerable loss in a fire at Great Barr, it was John Hoo, together with the Rector, who wrote to the surrounding parishes and invited them to take up a collection for the benefit of William Page. He took a lively interest in parish affairs, and his signature with that of his son often appears with those of the others who were present when the various parish officers had their accounts passed. In the church at Great Barr are still two silver patens and a chalice which he presented. When he died his heirs declined to have him buried in a woollen shroud as the law then required; instead they paid the appropriate fine, and John Hoo was buried in linen. He was succeeded by his son John, who died nine years later, to be followed by his brother Thomas.

Thomas Hoo was a confirmed bachelor, passionately devoted to foxhunting. He lived at the black and white Old Hall, where he kept his kennels well adorned with the trophies of the chase. It was said that he had once proposed marriage, but as the prospective bride took exception to his hounds, the marriage fell through for 'no woman was worth fifty hounds'. Henceforth women were forbidden entry to his bachelor's retreat where he was reputed to live in great affluence. He did condescend, however, to toast his one-time neighbour, Mrs. Galton, as 'the only reasonable woman in the world' and to tolerate the visits of her daughter, Ann, who as a child roamed over his estate. In 1772 he was high sheriff of Staffordshire and he also played his part in parish affairs, sometimes holding the unpaid office of Surveyor of the Roads. The Charity Commissioners when they visited this district some thirty years after his death commented in their report, on Mr. Hoo 'who managed all the charities in the neighbourhood'. His funeral in 1791 was long remembered for the large procession which followed the coffin from Barr to Aldridge Church. The Hoos were good lords of the manor, being interested in the people and in the district, and playing their part in the life of the community.

The charities which Thomas Hoo managed would be those bequests usually associated with the church, whereby some people had left small incomes in the form of rents to be given to the poor either as money payments or in some other form. Usually, oversight of a charity was given to the Rector and Churchwardens. On the west wall of Aldridge Church hangs a wooden box in which were placed each Sunday six penny wheaten loaves to be given after the service to such of the aged poor who attended both service and sermon. Thomas Davill had left twenty-six shillings per annum from property in Bosty Lane, for this to be done. Similarly, John Cox left five shillings per annum rent arising from land at Walsall Wood where the Boot Inn stands; whilst Mrs. Walker left £100 to buy land, the rents to be given to ten poor houskeepers each year on St. Thomas's day. Ten other charities at Aldridge yielded sums ranging from five shillings to forty-two shillings each. Part of John Jordan's charity was somewhat different. He provided ten shillings per annum for Bibles and Prayer Books to be given on Easter Monday to 'such poor children as can read and who usually attend divine service'. Others provided for payments to the Parish Clerk and to the Schoolmaster. The charities were referred to collectively as 'Coxe's Dole' and were usually distributed on St. Thomas's Day and on Good Friday. On May 23rd, 1697, the Rev. John Jordan distributed twenty-two shillings and sixpence of this money to eleven recipients in the Parish Church. In 1827, £4 19s. 0d. was distributed on Good Friday and £2 16s. 6d. on St. Thomas's day; seventy-five payments being made, ranging from one shilling to two shillings and sixpence each. Thomas Page and Sutton Page, however, received only one shilling and sixpence between them, and against the latter's name on the list of recipients appears the note 'an impudent woman'.

At Great Barr were similar charities; amongst them was provision for twenty-four penny loaves to be distributed on alternate Sundays in Church, and £5 annually for clothing to be given to four elderly women. These usually received a gown, apron, shawl, bonnet, two pairs stockings and a pair of gloves each, but there were some variations to make up the £5 exactly.

There was a real danger that the payment of these charities might be overlooked, and in course of time the details forgotten and the charity lost. The people of Pelsall guarded against this, for on the north wall of the old church there was 'a rudely painted figure of an old man holding a purse in the left hand and money in the right, and underneath this inscription "Richard Harrison gave twenty groats to the poor of Pelshall to be paid yearly on New Year's Day. The land charged to pay the money is the Old Croft. Aged 101"'.

These charities did very little to relieve the poor, and many were desperately poor. The Poor Law provided for the raising of Poor Rates in each parish based on the value of property owned or leased and for the administration by the Churchwardens and the Overseer of the Poor of the money so raised. The latter was an unpaid official appointed annually by the ratepayers at the parish vestry meeting. The Overseer kept detailed accounts which were submitted to the vestry to be passed when the Overseer had served his term of office (twelve months) and a new Overseer was appointed. The accounts at Great Barr are more detailed than those at Aldridge, and the following extracts from Great Barr illustrate the work of the Overseer and conditions in the parish. Aldridge and Great Barr for Poor Law purposes were regarded as separate parishes.

1753 June 30 Paid for a pair of shoes for Welches wench........................1s. 8d
1754 December Paid for a skin for Robert Hill's breeches..........................6d
1755 Feb Pd Richard Blackbourn for fetching some pewter back as Ed.
    Shorthouse had taken to sell..1s. 6d
    Pd Ed Shorthouse reliefe..2s. 6d
1757 Jan For a load of coles for Wm Page...8s. 6d
    Apl Pd Page reliefe and washing him and mending his clothes..............4s. 6d
    June Pd ye surgeon for setting a child's arm and curing a burned face
      of ye child 10s. 0d
1758 Oct. Pd for nitting Hadley's son 2 pair stockings..............................6d

Those unable to work through age or infirmity received regular weekly payments, and there were many odd payments to relieve temporary distress without giving details of the cause. A birth or a death inevitably placed a strain on the family which could only be met by recourse to the Overseer. The following are typical of many other entries:

1752 Feb 28 Pd for looking after Fellows wife and relieving her in her
    lying in ....9s. 3d.
    Pd the midwife for laying her...2s. 6d.
1753 Charges about John Arrowsmith's funeral.................................2s. 6d.
    Paid for a shroud...3s. 6d.
    A coffin ....7s. 0d.
    Bread, Cheese and Drink..8s. 0d.
    Fees at Aldridge Church..3s. 10d.
    Bott. Jn Arrowsmith wine and other things in his illness....................4s. 4d.
    Pd for looking after him and laying him out.....................................2s. 0d.
    My own loss of time buying Shroud and attending funeral..................1s. 0d.

In the case of John Arrowsmith the parish were able to reclaim some of the money by the subsequent sale of his belongings. Bread, cheese and drink figure largely in most funeral expenses, suggesting that many attended the interment. More grim is the following entry:

1752 Charges burying the man that was hang'd in the Hays Rough and
    paying the jury and going for the Corriner more nor what was made
    of his clothes...12s. 6d.

The Overseer did not always call in a doctor to treat all cases of illness.

1775 Paid to George Bussey for 2 quarts of ale for Wheeley's wife...............8d.
    And quartern of brandy 6d. and ¼ pound shugger 1d............................7d.
1797 Treacle and Brimstone for Ash's family...................................1s. 0d.
    July 18 For curing Ash's family of the Itch (Scabies ?).......................10s. 6d.
    Dec. 30 Curing Baskervills of the Itch...1s. 0d.
    Mrs. (?) for curing Chattertons of Itch..2s. 0d.
1791 July 16 Thos. Worthington Expenses to Stafford for a wooden leg 3s. 0d.
1801 Oct. 9 Mending Ann Bedworth's Bed Pan ....3d.

On the whole, the parish seems to have treated the poor well compared with the treatment given in other parishes. There are frequent entries for 'coles' and others such as the following:

1759 Apl Pd for tobacco for Thos Standley..1s. 0d.
     Pd for plants and Taters for Greens wife to sett her garden with.................6d.
     July Bott tools for David Grice to set up with when he came of being
     a soldier ....12s. 0d.
1791 Apl 23 Pd for thatching and repairing the old house Smiths,
     Stringer, Johnson and Harpers live in at Queslett....................£3 9s. 0d.
     June 3 Pd Wid Wheeley for flax...1s. 6d.

Poor Rates were a big burden on the parish and at the close of the eighteenth century the cost of poor relief was rising rapidly. The census of 1801 shows that at Aldridge were 146 families giving a population of 736, whilst at Great Barr were 113 families, population 756. At a time when one shilling and sixpence was the approximate daily wage of a labourer, the two villages had to raise the following sums for poor relief:

Aldridge
1789	£157
1791	£179
1796	£261 (The year after the Enclosure Act granted)
1801	£384 (The year after the enclosures were completed)
1823	£502

Great Barr
1791	£109
1796	£182
1801	£364
1823	£431

It is not suggested that enclosure was the only cause for the increase in poverty. Agricultural wages were depressed throughout England and with the war with France, prices rose whilst wages were held steady or even declined. On the other hand the Wyrley and Essington Canal was cut during these years and should have brought temporary prosperity at least.

If enclosure was a prominent cause of the distress, those who profited most from the enclosure did least to relieve the poor. Under the award Mrs. Foley and Mrs. Whitby had received 632 acres, Joseph Scott 192 acres, Ann Scott 114 acres. In 1795, the year of the Enclosure Act, the levy book records that Mrs. Scott paid £11 poor rates, but there is no entry for Joseph Scott, Mrs. Foley or Mrs.

Whitby; presumably their property was all leased and their tenants had to pay.

Meanwhile the parish struggled on. How desperate things were can be seen from the entry in Great Barr accounts:

1801 Apl 30 Supply poor with flour one month........................£12 1s. 0d.

At Aldridge, houses owned by the parish had to be sold for £100 and arrangements made with Shenstone, for Aldridge poor to be accommodated when necessary in Shenstone workhouse. Some could not pay the poor rates due, as in September, 1818, when six Aldridge men appeared before the J.P.'s at Wednesbury for none payment of rates ranging from five shillings owed by Sam Parkes to £4 12s. 9d. owed by William Simkins.

It was the duty of the Overseer to see that the parish did not help anyone if another parish could be made responsible. All strangers entering the parish were examined and if there was any likelihood of their becoming a liability they were not allowed to stay. The poor were unable to move elsewhere in search of work. Eventually some parishes issued certificates accepting responsibility for the bearers if they fell in need of poor relief. This helped some people to move, but everywhere such certificates were closely scrutinised, whilst beggars and vagabonds were whipped and sent back to their home parishes.

Often the settlement was disputed, and then one parish would go to law with another. At Great Barr appear such entries as:

1759 Sept For going to Bromwich to appeal to ye order of Sarah
    Edwards & expenses ....1s. 6d.
  And for going with ye indenture to Sutton, Mr. Homer, myself &
    Mr. Osbourne. expence..1s. 6d.
  For going with Mr Homer's clerk to deliver ye subpanes and search ye
    register at Bromwich for ye paupers age........................2s. 2d.
    Pd for dinner & ale on same account..............................2s. 8d.
  Pd Mr. Homer for his trouble and retaining Counsel paying them and
    attending ye sessions at Stafford for Sarah Edward's tryall .... £10 0s. 0d.
  Pd witnesses and horsehire do...£1 5s. 0d.
  Myself & Clark going..4s. 0d.
  Expenses coming and going at Stafford & paid in court..............£1 9s. 8d.

Despite the settlement laws there were many travellers, as can be seen from the following entries in Aldridge Parish Register:

1725 Buryed Ann Midcock a Stranger June ye 1st.
1725 Buryed Charles Swinger a Passenger June ye 10th.
1726 Buryed James Hill a Stranger Jan 21st.
1727 Buryed Jane Roe a Traveller Nov. 4th.
1727 Baptised John the son of a travelling woman Feb 25th.
1728 Buryed a travelling boy Oct 14th.
1728 Buryed George Lylly a strange child Nov 2nd.
1728 Buryed A strange woman from Barr Dec. 3rd.
1728 Buryed a travelling man Dec 24th.

Members of the armed forces and their families could claim relief from parishes they travelled through to help them on their journey. It would be a brave Overseer who attempted to evade payment on occasions such as that at Aldridge in December, 1824, when eleven soldiers' wives with their incredible brood of eighty-one children, appeared simultaneously before the Overseer to claim relief to enable them to reach Tamworth. Their husbands had recently sailed, some for New South Wales and some for the Barbadoes. Their visit cost the parish £2 1s. 4d.

In the Aldridge Parish chest were preserved many papers relating to the poor and their settlements. Assuming that the poor told the truth when questioned, the following stories can be pieced together:

Catherine was born at Smithy Brook, near Manchester, about the year 1748. To that parish came one, Laurence Ashwell of Rochdale, and gained a settlement there. The two met, grew fond of each other, and when Catherine was but sixteen, they married. Laurence, possibly finding it hard to support his wife, but more likely because of the attitude of the parish who would fear a family of paupers, joined the army, enlisting in the 69th Regiment of Foot. Catherine then assumed the wandering life which was the common lot of soldiers' wives, following the Regiment up and down the country. When her husband was sent to Gibraltar she managed to follow. There, three years later, her husband died, leaving Catherine to fend for herself. Fortunately it seems there were no children. At this time the 12th Regiment of Foot was also in Gibraltar, and there Catherine found her second husband—Sergeant Thomas Smith. Some months later Smith was discharged from his Regiment and with Catherine and their six-month old daughter Ann, they sailed for Liverpool. At Liverpool, Smith sent Catherine and Ann on to Walsall, where he said he had his settlement, whilst he travelled on to

London in search of work. At Walsall Catherine was met by her brother-in-law, who assured her that her husband had only lived at Walsall by virtue of a certificate from Aldridge. He brought her to Aldridge and handed her over to Thomas Smallwood, Church-warden, who immediately gave her twopence relief. Thereafter, Catherine and Ann were a burden on the Parish. Catherine was repeatedly examined but stuck to her story and was able to prove the marriage at Gibraltar. Meanwhile news reached Catherine that Smith had arrived at London, had found another lady and apparently had no intention of returning here. It was 1775 when Catherine arrived in Aldridge, and she was still receiving regular payments from the Overseer (five shillings per week) as late as April 1814; soon afterwards her name disappeared from the Poor Law accounts. Also in the Parish chest, however, was another document which reads: '27 weeks relief due Oct 3rd 1829 £3 7 6. Settled for Catherine Smith W.S.' How the Overseers must have cursed that unfortunate marriage at Gibraltar, about which they could do nothing. The daughter Ann also received parish relief until she reached the age of seven, she was then sent as a parish apprentice to William Haines of Wednesbury, brickmaker, who was to "teach" her the art and mystery of housewifery. The parish paid Haines a premium of £3 13s. 0d. for him to take Ann off their hands.

Job Eccleston was bound apprentice about the year 1769 to Joseph Palmer of Aldridge, whom he served for ten years. Job then enlisted as a soldier and was later known to be married and living at Burton-on-Trent, although still in the forces, and so not gaining a settlement at Burton. In 1782 the parish officials at Stafford found Mrs. Eccleston here, and having questioned her sent her to Aldridge—where Job had his settlement by virtue of his apprenticeship. By 1789 Job appears to have left his regiment, for he with his wife and children then visited his brother at Northfield. One morning his brother woke to find the children still there but Job and his wife missing. The Northfield officials promptly dispatched the children to Aldridge. In 1817 the Birmingham officials found the missing pair here and sent them back to Aldridge also. In 1829 Job was described as being seventy-nine years old and living with his son, who was a chimney sweep in Shropshire. The son, who had a large family of his own had difficulty in supporting him and Aldridge allowed Job one shilling per week. The Shropshire officials wrote to Aldridge pointing out that Job was nearly blind and was bad on his legs. They claimed that in such cases they allowed three or four shillings a week and asked Aldridge to increase the allowance. Aldridge put it up to three shillings, but hearing that Job was not receiving it they wrote to the Overseer of the parish where he was living and through whom the allowance was paid, inquiring why it was not being paid to Job. It transpired that Job's son, wishing to buy a patent chimney sweeping machine, had borrowed the money from the parish on the understanding that the parish could keep the money from Aldridge as repayment.

The hardest cases were those where children were involved. A child took the settlement of the parents where known, otherwise it was regarded as belonging to the parish where it was born. An illegitimate child (and there were many) was sure to be a charge on the parish, and so the Churchwardens and the Overseer kept a keen eye on the local girls; anyone suspected of being in trouble was taken to a local Justice and questioned as to the father, when everything possible would be done to force them to marry, or failing that, to see the father paid all expenses. Sometimes the girl refused to name the father, and then it was the duty of whoever acted as midwife to question the mother at the time of birth. In the Aldridge chest was a very unpleasant document signed by Susanna Bullock in 1736. In it she tells how Elizabeth Branston, travelling from Derby arrived at the Bullocks' home, where she gave birth to a son. As Elizabeth refused to name the father, the midwife refused to perform her office, but the child lived and was given the name 'Richard Astonbrook'. One hopes that Susanna's statement was untrue and only made for the benefit of the parish officials.

In Great Barr accounts occur such entries as the following:

1791 May 23 Journey to Birm'm with Jane Cressall and to examine her
to settlement ....4s. od
Paid for a warrant for George Rutter..2s. od
24 A Journey to Aldridge to take him...3s. od
Expenses there 1s. 7d
For man and horse to Aldridge to fetch Mr Lomax (a local
clergyman) ....2s. od
Journey to Birm'm to examine Rutter to his settlement...................3s. od
Examination and expenses...4s. 3d

The above entries are from the Constable's accounts. The Poor Law accounts complete the story:

1791 May 24th Expenses, Wedding fees, Dinner, liquor etc at wedding
   of George Rutter and Jane Cressall..£1 2s. 9d.

The effort appears to have been in vain for later comes the entry:

1791 June 28 Jane Cressall's child 1 week pay......................................1s. 6d.

Weekly payments continued for the child for the next five years, after which comes the entry:

1796 Sept 2 Bindg J Cresswell's child to T. Cresswell............................2s. 6d.

A black sheep could cause the parish a lot of trouble and Aldridge had its share of black sheep. How such a one tried the parish can be seen from the following documents.

May 6, 1816 Certificate issued for the removal to Aldridge of Sarah Stackhouse "single and with child" from Pelsall.

Dec 3, 1817 Order made by a J.P. for John Masefield of Beckby to pay £5 13s. 6d. and 1/8 weekly for the child of Sarah Stackhouse.

July 22 1818 Order made for Francis Slater of Pelsall to pay £10 and 1/8 weekly for the child of Sarah Stackhouse.

April 3 1822 Order for the removal from Barton under Needwood to Aldridge of Sarah Stackhouse, single and with child.

One of the children apparently died, for the entry each week in the 1822 accounts is 'Stackhouse's 3 children 6/-'.

The parish could move with speed in these matters, as can be seen from the following:

June 17 1818 Deposition of Sarah Nixon that Sam Ashwood of Broseley is the father of her child.

June 17 1818 Magistrates order for Sam Ashwood to pay £3 14s. od. and 1/8 per week for Sarah Nixon's child.

June 17 1818 Certificate of the Overseer of the Poor at Aldridge that Sam Ashwood owes the parish £3 16s. od.

June 17 1818 Order to the Constable to commit Sam Ashwood to the House of Correction for failing to pay.

The parish had to arrange for all children to be looked after until they reached the age of seven. They could then be sent as parish apprentices. The parish do not appear to have been particular about the minimum age as can be seen from the details of Jane Cressall's child given above. The following is from the Great Barr accounts:

1751 July Pd Jno Wiggin with Sarah Leis apprentice......................£5 os. od.
 Pd for a bond to indemnify ye parish for her being under seven years
 of age & indentures & filling up... 10s. 6d.

A child thus bound had to serve his master until the age of twenty-four, or if a girl until twenty-one or marriage. The only return the child received for his labour was food, clothing, lodging and instruction in the master's craft, which was often a craft in name only. Small wonder that in 1777 it was necessary to pass an Act preventing the binding of boys after the age of twenty-one, since binding until twenty-four had been found 'to disturb the peace of domestic life, check marriage, and discourage industry', so the age was lowered 'to maintain the good harmony between apprentice and master'.

Preserved in the Aldridge chest were apprenticeship indentures dated between 1707 and 1836 for no fewer than eighty-eight boys and thirty-two girls. This is by no means the full total of parish apprentices for in the accounts is a list of premiums paid between November 1769 and January 1801. No indentures have survived for nineteen of the children for whom premiums were paid; and there are indentures for seven children for whom no premium was recorded. Ignoring those whose indentures have disappeared, it transpires that the boys were set to the following trades:

17 Farmers	3 Tailors	1 Pattern woodmaker
10 Bucklemakers	2 Chainmakers	1 Stirrup Ironmaker
8 Locksmiths	2 Butchers	1 Spurrier
5 Nailers	2 Forgemen	1 Gearmaker
5 Ropemakers	2 Stone miners	1 Staymaker
5 Platers	2 Bagustmakers (?)	1 Brassfounder
5 Bit makers	1 miner	1 Wheelwright
4 Blacksmiths	1 mason	1 Settmaker
3 Chapemakers	1 weaver	1 Cordwainer
		1 illegible

Eighteen of the boys were apprenticed in the parish—most undesirable from the officials' point of view, for if they were apprenticed elsewhere, their settlement would cease to be Aldridge. Most of these eighteen were apprenticed to farmers. Twenty-nine boys went to Walsall, seven to Birmingham, six to Willenhall, three to Great Barr and most of the others to villages within ten miles of Aldridge. All the thirty-two girls were to learn housewifery, save one to learn rope-making, one calico weaving, one farming, one frame wool knitting, and one who was apprenticed to a cotton factor at Lichfield to be employed 'as possible in his factory'. The girls were probably more difficult to place than the boys and no fewer than fifteen were apprenticed in Aldridge, where householders could be compelled to take them and where they probably made cheap servants. Of the rest seven were sent to Walsall, three to Birmingham, and one each to Longdon, Rugeley, Shrewsbury, Wednesbury, Measham (Derbyshire), Lichfield and Shalstone (Leicestershire). The premiums paid ranged from £1 11s. 6d. to £5, though £2 10s. 0d. was more usual; there was no difference between the premiums paid for boys or girls, age also does not seem to have affected the premium. The clause on the printed indentures whereby the employer was to provide new clothes at the end of the apprenticeship is erased from those indentures dated 1754 to 1762.

Many of these children were illiterate; those apprenticed at a distance would be completely cut off from friends and family and at the mercy of an unknown master. The law demanded that the apprentice should not be ill-treated, but there was no inspection to ensure this. Much as one would like to know how they fared there is no means of finding out, for having set them apprentice the parish regarded them as off their hands and took no further interest in them. Some probably ran away from their masters and *Aris's Birmingham Gazette* carries many advertisements asking for information about runaway apprentices, whilst in the Great Barr accounts appears:

1756 Charges for taking Welches daughter to Walsall when she had over run her master and brought to me by an order and maintaining her a day and a night at my house......................................1s. 6d.

A boy of eighteen or nineteen, capable of earning his own living, yet bound to work for a master until the age of twenty-one without wages, would be greatly tempted to abscond, but this was not always easy. John Jaycam of Norton Canes was bound as a parish apprentice in 1787 to Joseph Wiggin of Pelsall, nailer. In 1797 John ran off to Birmingham. There he found out the Recruiting Officer and joined the army, swearing he was not an apprentice. The army kitted him out and sent him to Shrewsbury, but his master had started inquiries and found out where he was. The master applied to the Quarter Sessions and the army were forced to hand John back to his master. The army had been at some expense in kitting him out and so instituted proceedings against John for obtaining £10 15s. od. from them on false pretences, swearing he was not an apprentice. The outcome is not known, but the case was due to be heard at Warwick Assizes during the summer of 1797 and the brief prepared for the crown is now in the Birmingham Reference Library. The possible penalties for his offence were fine and imprisonment, or pillory, or public whipping, or seven years transportation.

How children, other than illegitimate children, came to be set apprentice can be seen from the case of Rhoda Palmer. In December, 1798, Edward Palmer received help from the parish, being ill and unable to work. Weekly payments were made to him until February 1799, when the expenses of his funeral appear in the accounts and payments were made to his widow. On February 27th the parish vestry met and it was reported to them that his daughter, Rhoda, was then seven and so could be set apprentice. It was resolved that she should go to a Mr. R. Hollows. Clothing to the value of ten shillings was bought for Rhoda and early in April a premium of fifty shillings was given to Mr. Hollows. Mr. Hollows, however, seems to have passed the apprenticeship on, for Rhoda finally went to work for a Mr. Jewsbury, a calico weaver of Measham, and her apprenticeship indenture is made out to him. Calico weaving was then done by hand, usually in the damp atmosphere of a cellar. Little Rhoda, just seven years of age, a few weeks after her father's death was thus sent some thirty or so miles from Aldridge to work unpaid for the next fourteen years for a complete stranger, probably in a damp ill-lit cellar where she probably never again heard of anyone from Aldridge.

Such was the lot of the poor. Meanwhile, Joseph Scott, who was to become lord of the manor, was rebuilding and altering Nether

House, later to be known as Great Barr Hall (now St. Margaret's Hospital) in a most lavish fashion. A contemporary description of it appears in Cooke's *Warwickshire* (1800). It reads:

. . . the hospitable mansion of Sir Joseph Scott Bart. is surrounded by a park of considerable extent wherein there is the greatest variety of undulating hills and dales, woods and water, together with such extensive views as can only be found in this part of the kingdom. To this park there are three entrances, and at every avenue the worthy proprietor has erected an elegant lodge, from which there are capacious carriageways to the mansion. . . . On entering the park a circular coach drive leads to the holly wood, through which you proceed by a serpentine road near half a mile when a beautiful sheet of water presents itself to view, along whose banks you pass near a mile before you arrive at the mansion.

The situation of the building is low in front of the water, but being screened by rising ground and lofty trees, it must be very warm in winter. On the left of the house, a walk leads you to the flower garden which is laid out with great taste, containing flowers and small shrubs of the choicest and rarest kinds, together with a fountain in the centre. From here there are delightful views and among others over the adjacent country, Birmingham is distinctly seen. At a distance of about two miles further towards Walsall, there is another lodge which is the entrance from Walsall, and leads you by a spacious serpentine road through Marrion Wood which is composed of various shrubs and evergreens and conducts you to a most elegant chapel. . . .

There is another lodge at a place called the Queslet . . . where a spacious road conducts you for a considerable distance by a plantation of oaks and so through the park wherein there are fixed numerous seats which command delightful and comprehensive prospects.

Sir Joseph Scott, one-time M.P. for Worcester, was reputed to have squandered his way through three inherited fortunes, and was at one time reduced to leasing Great Barr Hall, on which he had lavished so much expenditure, to Mr. Galton the Birmingham industrialist, for twenty-one years. It was whilst Mr. Galton held this lease that the famous Lunar Society met at the Hall.

Sir Joseph Scott was captain of the Walsall Volunteer Association which was founded in 1798 during the war with France. It was a corps of cavalry of forty-three gentlemen; they received their colours at Barr Beacon on September 23rd, 1799. When the corps was disbanded in 1802 a silver cup, valued at fifty guineas, was presented to the captain for his services. It is usually assumed that this association was formed because of the threat of French invasion, but it was in 1803, after the association was disbanded that someone wrote in the church register at Great Barr, 'Bounaporte threatened England with Invasion 1803' and that threat reached its height in 1805. At this time there was no regular police force and riots were put down by the military helped by the Volunteer Associations. This Association was founded just when the enclosure of the local commons was almost complete and it was during its life (April, 1801) that the entry before referred to was made in the Great Barr accounts, 'Supply poor with flour, one month £12 1s. 0d.'. There were riots in other counties under similar circumstances, but there is no trace of any threat of rioting here. Had Sir Joseph misread the situation, or did he overawe possible rioters before they took action, or was the French war the real reason for forming the Association, and its members make the understandable mistake of assuming that the Peace of Amiens (1802) meant the end of hostilities?

BIBLIOGRAPHY

Finch Smith, *Notes and Collections of the Parish of Aldridge.*
Mary Anne Schimmelpenninck, Autobiography.
S.H.C., 1938.
Charity Commissioners, Reports, 1823 (Vol. 9), 1825 (Vol. 10).
C.R.O., Documents from Aldridge Parish Chest.
Aldridge, Parish Registers.
Great Barr, Parish Registers.
         Accounts still in Parish Chest.
Pitt, *History of Staffordshire*, 1817.
Cooke, *Warwickshire.*
B.R.L. (329318), Crown v. Jaycam.   Brief.
Aris's Birmingham Gazette.

CHAPTER IX

CHURCHES AND CHAPELS

THE CHURCH AT ALDRIDGE was probably founded about 1250 by Nicholas de Alrewych. The defaced effigy lying in the chancel is believed to be his, although there is no inscription. When Erdeswick wrote his *History of Staffordshire* (about 1600), the effigy then lay in an alcove outside the chancel wall and an inscription may have been legible, for Erdeswick was definite in his statement that it represented Nicholas. The structure was probably in local limestone, as a portion of the tower still is, though the tower was probably added during the fourteenth century. Great Barr Chapel was probably erected about the same time as Aldridge Church, for in 1257, Walter Suel of Kidderminster made provision for the maintenance of a glowing light before the altar of St. Michael in Barr Chapel. In the records of Pope Nicholas's taxation, granted to Edward I in 1288 to help meet the cost of a crusade, appears the entry 'Alrewych cum Capell X marc'—Aldridge (church) with (Great Barr) Chapel ten marks. Prior to the creation of Aldridge parish, this district was probably included in Handsworth parish.

The first church at Rushall was erected sometime before 1220 and its history has been traced in detail by Willmore in his *Records of Rushall*; a church at Pelsall was built in 1311 or earlier, for in that year William le Keu endowed it with land for the maintenance of a priest; perhaps to expatiate the murder of Henry de Norton which had been committed eight years earlier.

The earliest surviving documents in the churches are the Registers. As previously stated, the earliest surviving Aldridge register commences with entries dated 1660; but at Great Barr are entries made a few years earlier, during the Interregnum. At that time the entries were made not by the parish priest, but by a secular 'Register'— William Lucas, who was instituted by Sir John Wyrley, J.P., on

September 26th, 1653. Marriages were then secular, being performed by a magistrate, although the banns had to be called in a public place —usually the church. The marriage entries consist of a declaration that the banns had been called and the dates when this was done; then follows a signed declaration by the Justice that he has declared the couple to be man and wife. The banns were not always called in church. When John Weston and Margaret Bust were married, William Lucas recorded that the banns had been called 'three several market dayes at Walsall Market'.

At this period the interiors of the churches were probably white-washed, covering up any Elizabethan texts, etc., that may have adorned the walls. Finch Smith has described how during alterations to the Aldridge church, such texts were found on a wall previously covered up. The same author has described the church as it was prior to 1841. The chancel was longer than the nave and had a slightly lower roof. This difference in roof level can still be seen although the nave has now been lengthened to include part of what was the chancel. The south aisle was shorter than the north aisle and the arches on each side of the nave were odd, the arches have since been changed but are still odd. The floor of the church was covered with high-backed pews, facing in various directions, and were regarded as belonging to specific families. When John Jordan wished to change pews with Ann Wilcox (April 5th, 1736), a formal agreement was drawn up in writing and placed in the Parish Chest. There was scarcely any accommodation for the poor who did not have their own pews. Over the north aisle was a gallery with benches erected for the boys and the singers. There the boys were out of sight of both clergyman and congregation. The girls occupied benches placed beneath another gallery which stretched across the belfry arch.

Not only was the church closely associated with local charities but often collections were taken for deserving causes on receipt of what came to be known as a 'brief.' A few of these briefs were recorded in the registers where entries such as the following are to be found.

Collected for the ransom of Christian slaves out of Turkish slavery the sum of one pound three shillings and fivepence. November ye 19th 1671

August 2nd 1665 Collected for the relief of those that are visited by the plague five shillings fourpence

1701 Collected for the cathedral at Ely seven shillings fourpence

The collecting of money by briefs was later organised by firms of 'undertakers'. In the Aldridge chest was a printed receipt signed by 'T Lonsdale, Collector' for nineteen shillings and twopence raised in response to ten different briefs. At Great Barr, instead of a collection in church, a house to house collection was sometimes undertaken. Also in the Aldridge chest were a receipt for £8 4s. 0d. raised for British prisoners in France and dated May 7th, 1811; and two receipts dated 1847 for £29 and £4 8s. 0d. raised for the relief of the poor in Ireland and Scotland.

The Churchwardens were responsible for the maintenance of the fabric of the church; Great Barr had their own Chapelwardens. Some of their accounts have survived and from these it appears that the clock at Aldridge was installed prior to 1754 and that in 1771 Richard Griffis was in receipt of an annual salary of ten shillings to keep it in repair. After the turn of the century five shillings per week was paid to Thomas and Francis Sedgwick to teach the boys and girls to sing. The five bells in the Aldridge belfry (cast 1738 by Ab. Rudhal of Gloucester, probably at the instigation of the rector, Rev. John Dolman) were rung on national occasions. In 1772 the ringers sent in a bill to the Churchwardens for ringing on nine special occasions including the Restoration (May 29th) 2/6; Powder Plot (November 5th) 7/6; and Easter Monday 1/-. A bill dated 1829 for fourteen shillings and sixpence is for ale supplied to the ringers during the previous nine months. At Great Barr and Rushall similar bills were met. There is reference in the Great Barr accounts to William Meek, who is described as 'Dog Whiper' and who received a salary of twelve shillings per annum. A Dog Whipper's job was not to keep dogs out of church, but to see that those brought in behaved. Offenders were usually removed with the help of a pair of wooden tongs still to be found in some churches. Later, William Meek's title was changed to 'Beadle' and he was provided with a uniform. He also performed such tasks as clearing the snow from the churchyard. The churchwardens were responsible for exterminating vermin within the parish. In the Great Barr accounts appears such entries as:

1785 Oct. 16th   Katching 2 moles ....4d.
1818 July   Sparrowheads ....£1 2. 2d.
      August   Sparrowheads ....5s. 0d.
      Nov. 13   Sparrowheads ....2s. 6d.
      Dec. 25   Sparrowheads ....3s. 0d.

At Rushall there were many payments for hedgehogs.
  Other interesting entries in the Great Barr accounts are:

1784 Nov 10 For a proclamation for a general Thanksgiving for
  puting an end to the late extended and expensive war with America......2s. 0d.
1786 Jan 14 For repairing the churching seat and others.......................18s. 0d.
1818 March By two skins of parchment..10s. 6d.
1820 Dec 9 By Dixons bill for lead at Chapel.............................£2 14s. 8d.
1821 Jan 1 pd 2 men for watchg in the chapel in order to detect those
  who stole the lead ....10s. 0d.
1824 April 13 — 6 Halters for Chapel stable ....4s. 6d.

New bells were hung at Great Barr in 1796.

1796 Scales and weights to weigh the old bells & trouble and turnpike
  expense ....10s. 6d.
  Assistance of man and self to take down old bells............................5s. 0d.
  Bread cheese and ale for the men..3s. 2d.
  Taking bells to Birmingham & expenses.....................................£1 1s. 0d.
  My trouble how they were to go to Leicester and expenses..................2s. 6d.
  Expenses at Mr. Moore's twice when the bells came. 5 horses 2 men
    dinners, hay corn ale...14s. 3d.
  Expenses of Bell hangers and ringers at opening the Bells at Barr
    Wake ....£1 1s. 0d.
  Unloading the new and loading the old bells...................................9s. 0d.
  Ale at the Chapel at different times..3s. 6d.
  Carriage of the bells ....£13 18s. 3d.

The six new bells were cast by Edward Arnold of Leicester and
bear the names of Mary Whitby, Joseph and Margaret Scott and their
three children, William, Edward Dolman, and Mary.

During the eighteenth century, it was the custom of the Rector
to welcome on Christmas Day as many of his parishioners as cared
to call at the Rectory, and to give them as much bread, beef, mustard
and vinegar as they could eat. The origin of the custom is not known
but it must have been well established for it was looked on as one of
the village charities, and when a rector discontinued the custom, he
instituted a money payment instead, sixpence to each housekeeper
in Aldridge and eightpence to each housekeeper at Great Barr.

The Charity Commissioners were scathing about church matters when they visited Great Barr. Their report of 1825 refers to land which had been left to the parish to help pay the salary of a parish clerk. Sir Joseph Scott at the time of the enclosures had secured this land in exchange for land awarded to him on Barr Common. The exchange was fair except that no account had been taken of the timber, worth £112, growing on the land previously owned by the parish. The Commissioners claimed that Sir Joseph should answer for this money, together with the loss in value of land that had deteriorated in value because of the negligence of Sir Joseph's tenants. Sir Joseph declined to pay, pointing out that he had already spent £1,750 freely on the chapel. The Commissioners retorted that this money had been spent by him on six bells, an organ, stained glass windows, spire, battlements, porch, altar pieces, pulpit cloths, velvet and gold cushions, etc., whilst the more essential work of new pews, repairs to the chapel, etc., had only been achieved by borrowing £523 from a chapel warden (John Fallowes) and by leasing some of the clerk's land for a period of ninety-nine years in order to repay £220 of the money to Mr. Fallowes—a *bona fide* transaction, but one regarded by the Commissioners as improvident.

Sir Joseph Scott was also criticized on several other scores. His steward denied any trace of authority for a dole which used to be paid on Shustock Meadows, which Sir Joseph then held. He had also secured from the schoolmistress for £30 the house which she occupied, but to which she had no title. It was not clear whether this house ought to belong to the parish or to Sir Joseph as heir of the Hoo family. The Parish Clerk's house had also been secured under dubious circumstances. The house was originally provided for the Parish Clerk to live in, but a Richard Grove who had been Clerk, refused to surrender it. The trustees brought an ejection order against him, but it failed, and the trustees then filed a bill in Chancery claiming Grove had committed perjury. Before the case was heard Grove died, whereupon Sir Joseph, who had been one of the trustees trying to regain the house for the parish, bought it from the widow for £110 and installed one of his labourers. The action against Grove cost the parish well over £200, though Sir Joseph gave £41 to help meet the cost of the action.

The living at Aldridge was a valuable one and the patronage was normally in the hand of the lord of the manor of Great Barr. When the living fell vacant Sir Joseph granted it to a non-resident, John Dudley, who was to occupy it until Sir Joseph's son, William, should be old enough. William Scott held the living from 1821 until 1829, and it was he who had the present rectory built. The autocratic Rev. Henry Harding followed, and appears to have commanded considerable respect in the parish. His wife was the Lady Emily Fielding, sister of the seventh Earl of Denbigh. On his resignation the living was divided, Great Barr becoming a separate parish (1849). The living at Aldridge was then worth £628 and that of Great Barr £770, most of the money being from tithe rents which have tended to decrease over the years despite the value of money decreasing also.

The first rector of the reduced parish of Aldridge was a man of character, Rev. J. Finch Smith, M.A., F.S.A., son of the High Master of Manchester Grammar School; a gentleman who took his work as rector very seriously and who published two volumes, *Notes and Collections of the Parish of Aldridge*. These give many interesting details of some of the people who lived in Aldridge during the early nineteenth century but unfortunately they are a little inaccurate when referring to earlier periods. His great work was the rebuilding of the north aisle and chancel of the parish church, and the restoration and improvement of the rest of the building. He himself contributed £250 towards the total cost of £1,036. The church was re-opened on June 2nd, 1853, in the presence of the Bishop of Lichfield, who conducted the morning service. The rector has described how the villagers observed that day as a general holiday, and how 170 people, including the workmen, sat down at midday to a public luncheon in one of the glebe fields. A further service was held in the evening. The rector was also instrumental in securing most of the stained glass windows that now grace the church and had strong views about ugly and inappropriate headstones.

In 1851 a Wesleyan chapel was opened in Walsall Wood Road. A very different building to the venerable church, and an abomination to the rector, not on aesthetic grounds, which would have been understandable, for it was built in blue brick, but because he had no room for Nonconformists and their preachers. He alone was responsible for the cure of the souls of his parishioners. In 1850, when funds were being raised for this chapel or 'meeting house', as the rector preferred to call it, he issued a printed booklet of some fourteen pages. It was called 'Church—not Meeting House' and it began:

A meeting house is being erected in our parish, and I am told, will shortly be used on Sundays, and perhaps at other times for preaching and extemporary prayer. It is an unhappy reflection that any member of the church should have been found here willing to give even sixpence towards the foundation of that which cannot be, at the best, anything but the cause of strife and dissension amongst us.

One hopes that the Methodists did not retaliate by hampering the Rector's efforts to raise funds for the Parish Church alterations. The ill-feeling between church and chapel grew, and later in the century the local press carried letters complaining that Noncon-formists were barred from the local charities and even from the village school (originally a 'Free Grammar School') unless the children also attended the Anglican Sunday School. This issue divided the village. As a result of a petition to him, the People's Warden, Dr. Cooke, in 1869 called a Vestry meeting to discuss the affairs of the school, placing a notice to that effect on the Church door. The curate's 'friendly' letter to him asking him to remove the notice was without effect, but on the day of the meeting when Dr. Cooke sent the sexton to the Rector for the key of the Church, the Rector refused to hand it over, claiming a Vestry meeting could not discuss the affairs of the school. Consequently the meeting adjourned to the Elms Inn. There the Rector was strongly criticised for refusing the church key to the People's Warden, but the Rector's Warden, Mr. F. F. Clarke, defended the refusal. The meeting was a somewhat stormy one and dissatisfaction was expressed with the appointment of the Trustees of the school and the imposition of a religious test. Anxiety was expressed that the School should be brought under the Endowed Schools Act when no religious test would be possible. Happily, this strife is now long dead and when the present Wesley Hall was opened in 1936 the then Rector (Rev. Cooper) was able to join in the Methodist celebrations.

The Rev. Finch Smith's swansong was the sermon he preached in the Church on Whitsunday, 1878, and which was later printed. In it he looked back over the years, noting the various changes; once only one stained glass window, but now eleven; the introduction of a surpliced choir; more reverent behaviour in church, a better knowledge of scripture, a keener sense of the duty of churchmanship; an awareness of the sin of schism; the willing giving of alms, etc. One may disagree with the Rector's intolerance, but his energy and sincerity demand respect.

The story of Nonconformity in the village is rather obscure, for lamentably, Nonconformists seldom keep or preserve records conscientiously. Mention has already been made of the Presbyterian Leigh influence at Rushall, and significantly soon after the Restoration (1660) the vicar of Rushall (Richard York) and the curate of Pelsall (William Wilson) were ejected from their livings. At the back of the Aldridge Parish Register is the note 'A register of ye births of such children whose parents dissent from ye Church of England and wch we are ordered to register pursuant to an Act of Parliament made in the sixth and seventh year of William ye third'. Then follows a list of twelve children born between 1696 and 1724 belonging to the families of Richard Bell, Charles Fielding, John Hamnett, John Williams, and Thomas Dale. Richard Bell may have been the minister (or his son) of that name who was ejected as a Presbyterian from the living of Polesworth, near Tamworth, who had been licensed in 1672 to preach in the houses of Richard Eves, George Fowler, and Elizabeth Deale of Walsall. In 1704 the following houses were certified at Quarter Sessions as places of worship under the Toleration Act:

House of Richard Bell, Yeoman, Kings Haies, Aldridge.

House of William Asplyn, yeoman, Coppy Leasowes, Aldridge.

In 1745 there were probably Methodists in Aldridge, as the following extract from *Aris's Birmingham Gazette* shows. The paper is referring to riots at Wednesbury when Methodists there were attacked and much of their property damaged:

They served some people at West Bromwich and Aldridge in the same manner ; but the Goods they took from Aldridge were forced from them by the Walsall People as they were bringing them to that Town, and restor'd to their proper Owners. A great part of the rest of the Goods taken from different Places, the Mob were prevailed on by the most considerable People of Darlaston and Wednesbury to lodge in a House in Darlaston, that the Proprietors might come and lay Claim to them ; so that it is to be hoped that they will make no more Attempts of this Kind.

The neighbouring Gentlemen'did all they possibly could to make them desist, by giving them Drink, offering them Money, and using every other means they thought might have any Effect.

Accounts from Methodists' sources are rather more lurid but add nothing to our knowledge about Methodists at Aldridge.

In 1745 also, Francis Asbury was born at Hamstead and soon afterwards came to live at Great Barr. There he was sent to school but came to loathe the Master, who he said treated him with great severity. At the age of thirteen he was apprenticed to a smith, a Mr. Foxall, who was a friend of the family. At fourteen, dissatisfied with the services at Great Barr Chapel, he attended All Saints, West Bromwich, where he heard many evangelical preachers. Later he went to Methodist meetings at Wednesbury and was converted during the summer of 1760. Despite his tender years, he rapidly became a Methodist Class Leader and a Local Preacher of great popularity. In 1767 he was admitted 'on trial' as an Itinerant Preacher, but in 1771 volunteered to go to America. At the age of thirty-nine he was ordained by Dr. Coke as Joint Superintendent or Bishop of American Societies. In America he is reputed to have travelled 250,000 miles on horseback, preaching wherever needed. When he died at the age of seventy, the Methodist Church in America could boast of 218,000 members. He is one of the greatest figures in American Methodism.

A Methodist Society is reputed to have met in his mother's house at Great Barr and a chapel was built there early in the next century. These Great Barr Methodists were alert, for when a Bill was before Parliament in 1811 which might have affected the toleration they enjoyed, forty-seven members drew up and signed a petition to the 'Lords Spiritual and Temporal' against the Bill. By 1817 Methodists were meeting at Daw End (Sundays, 11 a.m. and 2-30 p.m.) and Pelsall (Sundays, 6 p.m.), which were included in the Wednesbury circuit. By 1845 Sunday meetings were also being held at the Hardwick (2-30 p.m.) and Aldridge (6 p.m.), and by 1862 there was a Methodist Day School at Pelsall. By this latter date the Hardwick meeting had been superseded by meetings at Barr Beacon (3 p.m.) and Mill Green (6 p.m.). The circuit plan for 1862 shows the typically early Methodist 'Love Feasts' were still being held quarterly at Aldridge and Pelsall. Where the Aldridge Methodists met before the chapel was built in Walsall Wood Road (1850) is not known. The Primitive Methodists had a meeting in Stubbers Green, where the Anglicans also held services. In 1890 these Primitive Methodists opened the chapel in Leighswood Road (now a potato crisp factory) and there was then rivalry between Wesleyan and Primitive Methodist as well as between Anglican and Nonconformist. The Congregationalist Chapel at Rushall was built in 1860, mainly as a result of the exertions of Mr. Alfred Stanley, who had organised meetings over the two preceeding years.

BIBLIOGRAPHY

Erdeswick, *History of Staffordshire.*
H.M.S.O., Calendar of Close Rolls 1257 (p. 145).
S.H.C. 1911, VII (1).
Great Barr Register.
Aldridge Register.
Finch Smith, *Church—Not Meeting House.*
          Notes and Collections of the Parish of Aldridge.
C.R.O., Churchwardens' Accounts, Aldridge.
Great Barr Chest, Churchwarden's Accounts.
Charity Commissioners, Report 1825.
Walsall Free Press.
B.R.L. (205407) Petition to Lords Spiritual & Temporal.
Aris's Birmingham Gazette.
Briggs, *Bishop Asbury.*
A. G. Matthews, *Congregational Churches of Staffordshire.*

CHAPTER X

THE VILLAGE CONSTABLE

THE PARISH CONSTABLE'S TASK was onerous, for he was the executive officer at the beck and call of the other parish officials. Often the more disagreeable tasks fell to him. His office carried no salary (save an honorarium of five shillings per annum) and any robust villager of good repute was liable to be chosen at the Court Leet and obliged to fill the office for the following twelve months At Great Barr the work became too much for one man, and so the Constable was given an assistant with the title 'Headborough'. Some men appear to have enjoyed the office, for they continued as Constable or Headborough (often alternately) year after year, as did Nathaniel Hathaway and Gilbert Haughton (innkeeper). Normally, the Constable was chosen from amongst the smaller farmers, innkeepers and more reliable labourers—men not chosen for the offices of Churchwarden, Overseer, or Surveyor of the Roads. The badge of office was the staff which the Constable carried each year at the wakes as a sign of authority and a warning to possible wrongdoers. Occasionally the Constable was illiterate and that must have caused considerable trouble, especially in the keeping of accounts. The Constable's accounts at Great Barr go back to 1714 and give a vivid picture of the work of the Constable and some of the matters which affected the life of the villagers. The following are typical of many entries and show the Constable assisting the Overseer, dealing with and relieving travellers:

1714 Nov 7 Pd for relieveing two meined shoulders by pass bound to
Chester ....6d.
June 5 pd for relief of 2 seamen goin to Liverpool...................................6d.
1745 For Maintaining 17 vagrants all night..5s. 8d.
1751 Given 3 disbanded sailors wounded by Turks............................1s. 6d.

1784 Expence of a poor man taken upon the Common in the cold
   weather ....1s. 10d.
1817 Relived Irishman with pass...3d.
   To relief Blackman ....2d.

Besides soldiers and sailors, there were many others travelling the roads, including expectant mothers, the latter especially in 1755 if the accounts are to be believed. These were helped and hurried on their way with a minimum of delay, and no doubt, with the full approval of the Overseer and the ratepayers, who would be anxious that no new child should gain a settlement by being born in the parish. The Constable was expected to maintain the peace, prevent robberies, arrest and hold offenders until they could be brought before a Justice, convey people to gaol or workhouse as needed, and in addition maintain the stocks, the pinfold, the horseblock and even the bridges. Hence such entries as the following were made:

1714 March 31 For a hew and cry after Landen......................................4d.
1716 June 28 Paid for mending the stox...2s. 6d.
1786 Expenses for settling the peace between Thomas Reeves and John...1s. 3d.
1820 July 18 Pd for a pair of handcuppols..5s. 0d.
1829 June 22 Pd for 1 sett of legg chains.......................................£1 3s. 6d.

He also assisted in the levying of taxes.

1714 Aug 9 Pd ye Sessors of ye Land Tax...3s. 0d.
1720 Sept. for chusing a collector for ye Window Tax...........................2s. 0d.
1791 Nov 17 Expenses at Justices meeting with Hair Powder List............5s. 0d.

The common was a source of continual trouble; not only did the Constable have cases like those already referred to of firing the ling and catching rabbits, but he was continually (after 1820) breaking up gypsy camps and moving the gypsies on. The Common was also an ideal place for the illegal Prize Fights (and Cockfights when they also eventually became illegal). Prizefights attracted big crowds and the Constable would have little chance of preventing the sport. Nevertheless, there is the following entry:

1825 Attending at the Common to prevent a fight...............................3s. 0d.

By that year, the Common was enclosed, so presumably the fight was in one of the fields, though tradition has it that the gravel pit which was at the junction of Longwood Road and Barr Common Road was often used as a ring, the spectators standing round the top of the pit and looking down on the contestants.

All the land (open common until 1799) stretching from the top of Barr Beacon to Sutton was referred to as Sutton Colefield, and somewhere on this waste there assembled on one occasion a crowd well over a thousand strong. There were strangers from as far afield as London who had come to see a fight in which the great Tom Belcher himself acted as second. The fight lasted four hours (213 rounds) before finally the contestants (Griffiths and Bayliss) were persuaded to both give in and call it a draw.

The Constable also visited public houses, checked weights, and kept a record of lunatics. Even recusants and Sabbath observance fell under his purview.

1720 Sept 26 for taking ye Ale sellers to the Bors hed...........................1s. 0d.
1810 Feb 23 Delivery five summonses in Barr concerning short
weights etc. ....2s. 6d.
1835 Sept 7 Delivery lunitick list..1s. 0d.
1717 Nov 4 Pd for a presentment against ye Popish recusants...................9d.
1832 Nov 4 Expenses at Magistrates meeting of Witness to persecute
Higgins and Archer for breaking the Sabbath...................................6s. 0d.
Nov 15 Noticing Abram Parkes and Rostil from selling things on
Sundays ....2s. 0d.

The biggest trouble at one period was with the Militia and finding men for the forces. Early in the eighteenth century this work does not figure largely in the accounts, save for such entries as:

1714 Oct 4 pd John Harrison for sharping ye Town pikes.......................4d.
1715 Feb 21 Pd at Lichfield at ye meeting of foot soilders ye sum............3s. 0d.
1720 Sept. for steeling of the pikes...1s. 2d.

After 1757 the central government tightened matters up considerably and in 1766 issued orders for the assembling and ordering of the Militia, but at Great Barr the entry was made:

1767 May 12 Pd ye High Constable on account of not raising ye
militia for 1766 ....£8 12 3¾d.

In 1779 men were pressed into the army, and one can imagine the excitement there must have been in the village before there were such entries as follow. 'Tending' is equivalent to 'watching' or 'guarding':

1779 March 4 3 journeys to Justice Carlin's concerning 2 impressed men ....3s. 0d.
March 13 Pd Ralph Ivens for tending one night...............................1s. 0d.
    Pd Sam Parkes for tending 1 day & 1 night...................................2s. 0d.
    Pd Jno Bellinson for do...2s. 0d.
    Pd for drink   ....12s. 6d.
    Pd for eating   ....2s. 6d.
March 15 Pd for 2 days more eating & drincking............................4s. 6d.
    For ye overseer tending 1 day...1s. 0d.
    For ye Chapelwardens man tending 1 night...............................1s. 0d.
March 17 Pd for eating and drinking before start to search.................3s. 0d.
March 18 For ye Overseer tending 1 day......................................1s. 0d.
March 20 Pd for eating and drincking for tender of a man that was imprest   ....14s. 6d.
    Pd ye tenders for 1 night & 2 days on do....................................4s. 0d.
    for ye Chapelwarden and Constables journey to Stonnal..................2s. 0d.
    pd for 2 presentments..1s. 6d.
Apl 3 for ye expenses of ye 4th & 5th men that were imprest and tenders 3 days & 4 nights & settling accounts on Easter Monday...£1 12s. 4d.
and for Chapel Warding man Francis Clark, Jno Bellinson, Ross's man and self for loss of time...11s. 0d.

Later, the Constable had periodically to draw up a list of men liable to serve in the Militia, and then names were selected from the list of the person(s) to represent the parish in the army; the unfortunate could avoid serving by payment of a stipulated sum. Perhaps that explains the Club referred to in the accounts.

1810 Aug 14 attending a deputy Lieuts meeting Shenstone for ballot of O C Militia...6s. 0d.
    Aug 17 Journey round the parish to persons liable to the ballot to inform them of a Club being held at the Pig by order of the deputy Lieut   ....5s. 0d.
Sep 2, 3, 4. Journey to Evesham . . . (?) . . . for the purpose of takeing Josh Wixhey, a deserter but could get no intelligence of him..........£3 7s. 9d.
22 Attendg a Deputy Lieutenant's meeting Shenstone for second ballot of militia in lieu of Joseph Wixhey deserted............................6s. 0d.

More encouraging is:

1813 March 19 Pd 11 volunteers for local militia..........................£23 2s. 0d.
Paid doctor for examining the same...11s. 0d.
Pd for ale & 2 Sergeants for 2 men...4s. 8d.

BIBLIOGRAPHY

Great Barr Parish Chest, Constable's Accounts.

EDUCATION AND POLITICS

CHAPTER XI

COMPARED WITH SOME PARISHES Aldridge was fortunate, for as early as 1718 a Free Grammar School was built here. The brick building consisted of some two sitting-rooms, a schoolroom, kitchen, back kitchen and four upper chambers, the schoolmaster living on the premises with his wife, who at one period taught a small class of girls. The master was allowed to take paying boarders. The building, since converted into two cottages, still stands opposite the Rectory and between the Church and the present Endowed Boys' School; a very convenient situation, for the master was usually parish clerk also. In front of the school were sixty perches of land which served as garden for the master and as playground for the children.

The Rev. Thomas Cooper gave the land, described as being seventeen yards by eight yards, and adjoining the 'Play Piece', to a trust of sixteen Aldridge Freeholders (including the Rector) for a school to be erected, where Aldridge children would be taught the Anglican catechism, English and Latin tongues and the writing of English. The trustees were to have power to appoint or dismiss the master and when their number had been reduced by death to five, a new trust was to be formed, but all the trustees were to be free-holders and inhabitants of Aldridge. Meanwhile, thirty other men, including the dissenter, Richard Bell, had subscribed £48 to build the school and to meet the cost of enclosing waste land for the maintenance of the master. Finally, the Rev. John Jordan, lord of the manor of Aldridge, also endowed the school with approximately sixty-five and a half acres of waste which had been marked out into fields ready for enclosure. This endowment was increased when the trustees as landowners received a further allotment of waste when the rest of the commons were finally enclosed. To meet the cost of these latter enclosures, farmers were granted leases allowing them free use of the land for a period of years on condition that they enclosed the land and paid what fees were due to the Commissioners, etc. In 1822 the income from school land was £115 10s. od. per annum plus a further £2 per annum which had been left by a John Twyford to be paid annually to the master.

We know very little of the school in its early days. It probably played its allotted part fairly well, for no one seems to have bothered about the trustees until 1757 when there was only one still living and the trust was reformed.

In 1759 the following advertisement appeared in *Aris's Birmingham Gazette*:

At a large commodious room in the Free School at Aldridge in the county of Stafford (a place well-known for its healthful and pleasant situation) young gentle-men and others are taught the mathematical sciences particularly navigation or the art of sailing upon the sea, in one month, at four hours per day, by John Randles.

The syllabus appears to have departed radically from the original English, Latin and Catechism, or was it only paying boarders who learned navigation, certainly few residents of inland Aldridge would need it.

A later schoolmaster, William Tranter, was also Parish Clerk. He was the gentleman who erected the gallery in the church over the northern aisle for the boys and the singers. He was followed by a Mr. Stinton, in whose time half the spare land in front of the school was regarded as being the master's garden, the rest being the play-ground. The next master, Fairbanks, added to the garden a strip some seven or eight yards wide off the playground, whilst two later masters, Thomas Cook and Peter Edward Jackson both in turn enlarged the garden further at the expense of the playground, so that in 1822 the Charity Commissioners found the playground too small for the thirty-odd boys who attended and who were forced to use a small piece of land in front of the Rectory stables to which they had no right. Even the parents were complaining about this.

Thomas Cook also combined the offices of Schoolmaster and Parish Clerk. Some documents from the Parish Chest bear his beautiful copper-plate handwriting, but he appears to have been an irascible fellow who failed to perform his duties as master in a proper manner. Eventually the trustees became aware of this and tried to sack him, only to find Cook undismayed and defiant. He is reputed to have told them that:

... he should not leave the school, they had no more power to turn him out than they had to turn the parish church round, and they might each of them kiss his seat of honour only expressed rather more vulgar.

Cook contended that the trustees failed to fulfill the conditions laid down by the founders, who had stipulated that the trust must be reformed whenever there were only five remaining trustees, and that all trustees should be freeholders and inhabitants of Aldridge. At last the trustees got rid of Cook by giving him £40 per annum to retire peaceably whilst they appointed a new master, Peter Edward Jackson, at a reduced salary which was to be increased on Cook's death. The Charity Commissioners in 1822 commented on this arrangement, and the would-be village Hampden—Farmer Charles Juxon—used the arrangements as a stick with which to belabour the trustees. He pointed out bitterly that they were paying Cook for doing his job badly. Cook continued to hold the office of Parish Clerk.

When the Commissioners examined the Trustees in 1829 they apparently approved of them and of the school rules. These provided that all the sons of Aldridge people were to have free schooling between the ages of six and fourteen, save for eighteenpence each per quarter for pens, ink and copies to be paid by those who learn writing; and one shilling per annum for firing to be paid in advance by all. One wonders how many did not attempt to learn writing. Parents could buy their own books provided that they were such as the master desired to use, and the master, subject to the trustees' approval, could take boarders. The trustees had the right to expel irregular attenders. The syllabus then included reading, writing, arithmetic, Latin, and by voluntary agreement of the master, English grammar. The trustees apparently had been under fire, for in 1829 they issued a poster setting forth these rules, declaring that the Commissioners had been fully satisfied with them, and stating that they 'will oppose the interference of any person in the superintendence or regulation of the school' and that they 'denounce the right of all or any of the parishioners to direct or control them' but will 'with cheerfulness, attend to any complaints properly and respectfully made'. Two of the trustees, William Allport and Rev. William

Cowley, owned private schools; whilst the Rev. Cowley was also second master at Queen Mary's Grammar School, Walsall. In 1822 two of the free scholars were being taught Latin.

In 1833, Juxon issued a broadsheet addressed to the inhabitants of Aldridge. In it he asked whether any pupils had 'received a common education sufficient even for a tradesman', and alleged that ' while in England and the rest of Europe, the people are improving their minds and cultivating their understanding—are banishing the degrading Delusions of Ignorance and Superstition and are basking in the rays of Intellectual Light—this parish remains plunged in the scanty stock of Intellectual Knowledge which generally existed in the Seventeenth Century'. A few weeks later came a pamphlet on the same theme and referring to 'the wretched system of education therein practiced, the cruelties which are inflicted on the free boys and the tyranizing conduct of those persons who are officially engaged in the management of the charity'. In 1844 Juxon was still attacking the trustees, issuing yet another pamphlet, this time threatening to lodge a bill in Chancery.

At one time girls were allowed to attend the school and were admitted from the age of four and were taught by the master's wife. When Jackson was appointed in succession to Cook, this was no longer to be allowed. There was, however, a mysterious land endowment of £12 per annum believed to have been left by a Miss Wheeley to provide for the education of a few girls. In 1822, Thomas Cook's wife was teaching the girls whilst Mr. Cook received the £12. The Commissioners immediately recommended that the rector should collect the money and hand it personally to Mrs. Cook. They also noticed that the Girls' School allotment made when Barr Common was enclosed, was adjoining that of Sir Joseph Scott and was not sufficiently distinguished from it (the trustees' fault, not Sir Joseph's this time).

The method of choosing which girls should be taught can be gathered from the following notice which was nailed on the door of Aldridge Church and was later filed in the Parish Chest:

28 March 1830 Meeting to nominate poor girls between 6 and 10 years of which number Sir Edward Scott will appoint six to the free school known as Wheeley's charity.

by order of Sir Edward Scott Bart.

Charles Juxon's comments when he read that would have been illuminating.

At Great Barr also was a free school—the one at Snails Green which Francis Asbury had attended and where he claimed he was dreadfully bullied by the master. It was founded by a bequest of Thomas Addyes in 1722 and was for thirteen poor children to be taught English and writing. Nicholas Addyes added more land to the endowment in 1733, whilst Ann Scott left £400 to be invested for the school. This latter was invested in a mortgage on tolls on the Bromsgrove Road and brought in about £20 per annum. The number of scholars was then increased to twenty and were taught the three R's. They were expected to find their own books and writing material and as at Aldridge, were charged one shilling per annum for firing. Each scholar was clothed in a brown gown, a cap and a collar out of the charity, but sometimes there was only sufficient funds to clothe nineteen out of the twenty scholars.

In addition, at Great Barr was the house in the chapelyard referred to in an earlier chapter, where five poor girls were taught to read, write and sew. One room in this house was used as a vestry and Sunday School, but to the disgust of some of the parishioners, the schoolmistress was a Roman Catholic.

Besides the free schools there were a large number of private boarding schools, especially at the end of the eighteenth and beginning of the nineteenth centuries. Most must have been on a small scale, but there were two very notable exceptions—the schools at Cedar Court and Druid Heath.

Cedar Court was a young ladies' seminary, built by Mr. and Mrs. Allport, who previously had a school in Mill Green. Mr. Allport was also a surveyor. This was a select and flourishing concern, with at one time, as many as fifty boarders. The fees were high, £26 per annum for ordinary boarders, or fifty guineas per annum for parlour boarders. All scholars had to engage for one year and give a quarter's notice before leaving. No deductions were allowed for absence in winter. Each pupil was expected to provide two sheets, six towels and a silver tablespoon and teaspoon. The syllabus included grammar and needlework, but there were a number of extra subjects which could be taken on the payment of the following extra fees per quarter: Geography with globes, 10/6; French 21/-; Drawing

21/-; Dancing 21/-; Music 21/-. Further payments had also to be made for washing, whilst pens, etc., cost 10/6 per quarter.

The Druid Heath School was run by the Rev. James Lomax, erstwhile curate of Great Barr. His first school was at Coppy Hall, which he gave up because of illness. A prospectus he issued, described Druid Heath School as being 'a few hundred yards from Coppy Hall but far superior to it in point of salubrity'. He aimed at a general education fitting pupils for Commerce, the Professions, or the University. Besides the more usual subjects (Greek and Roman classics, French, English, Maths, Geography, etc.) pupils could learn Stenography, Navigation, Parabolics or Gunnery, and Astronomy. Pupils were expected to deliver periodic discourses themselves.

Himself suffering from poor health, Lomax devoted no fewer than seven paragraphs of the prospectus to health and diet.

Soon after rising a piece of Bread, Bread and Butter or in Summer mornings a small Draught of Milk will be offered to each : He is unwell from a permanent Cause or from transient Indigestion who refuses such Offers. At the Interval of an Hour, a Preparation of Milk will be served for Breakfast ; where Milk disagrees some other nutritive Fluid will be substituted : in any case Breakfast will not be allowed above Blood-heat — between Breakfast and Dinner some Refreshment will be offered to everyone. This will prevent Faintness, Internal Sinkings, Flatulency, and consequent Loathing of Food : too long Abstinence from Food is injurious, to the younger and feebler, materially so.

In due time Dinner consisting of a Reasonable Allowance of Butcher's Meat with Vegetables, will be served. It is only in the case of puny Children that an additional Quantity of Animal Food, with Beer, will be necessary. . . .

The school rules provided for morning and evening prayers and for regular attendance at church, prohibited visits to public houses, cottages, or other places in the neighbourhood 'where pupils might be drawn into expense or form improper connections' and forbade gambling, sporting with gunpowder, firearms or other weapons and the drinking of wines, spirits, etc., 'without the Knowledge of the Conductor of the School'. The terms were eighteen guineas per annum, but French, Drawing, Military Exercises and Fencing were extra. The prospectus has been reproduced in full by Finch Smith and there is an original copy in the Birmingham Reference Library. If the school can be judged by the success of the master's own sons, it was a good school; one son became a bookseller and publisher, one editor of the *Stockport Advertiser*, one a surgeon, and another a master at Halesowen Grammar School. Lomax died at the early age of fifty-seven, his pupils erecting his headstone in testimony to his 'unwearied attention to their welfare'.

Charles Juxon also has a headstone in the churchyard, but on his is the text 'Mark the perfect man and behold the upright, for the end of that man is peace'. Juxon spent most of his time marking the imperfect men in the parish, and his own life must have been far from peaceful. No doubt, he made many enemies but he did serve to keep parish officials on their toes, even if he was sometimes mistaken in his allegations. He was not born in Aldridge and his name first appears in 1826, when he subscribed ten shillings to the cost of the Town Pump (presumably this was the pump situated in Walsall Wood Road, near the junction with High Street). In 1827 he was Overseer of the Poor, whilst H. C. Allport of the Cedar Court Seminary, was Churchwarden. In February, 1827, they together called a meeting at the Anchor Inn to petition the legislation to continue the protection of Agriculture—Juxon was a farmer. As a farmer he also had to pay poor rates and in August, 1829, he wrote an angry letter to the Churchwardens and Overseer threatening to report them if they paid for the destruction of vermin out of Poor Rates, or paid for the altering of a well outside Coppy Hall (about which more anon). He also alleged that the vestry was very select. We do not know what sort of an answer he received, but in September he again wrote to the Parish officials demanding possession of a cottage leased to the parish or, he threatened, he would double the rent. A postscript added the explanation that the cottage was not fit to live in and he wished to rebuild it, but the letter, following the previous ones, suggests a desire to embarrass the officials.

By 1832 Juxon was no longer asking for the protection of agriculture, in fact quite the reverse. He was then chairman of the Aldridge Political Union, which was associated with the well-known Birmingham Union and had some Chartist sympathies. The Aldridge Union first met under Juxon's chairmanship on August 8th, 1832 with Mr. J. Fulford and Mr. Attwood (of Birmingham) present. A report of the meeting was published, celebrating the passing of the Reform Bill and calling for more reforms and for a wider franchise. Mr. Juxon's son moved at the first meeting:

that the enforced payment of Tithes and Church Rates is an act of moral injustice and oppression, and the council and Union do pledge themselves to make use of every legal and peaceful means within their power to abolish so flagrant an act of moral injustice.

That should have stirred up the Rector, who at that time was receiving annual tithe rents to the value of £1,098. In a poster published on September 12th, 1832, Juxon called for Parliaments of three-year duration, household suffrage, revision of Common and Statute Law, monetary reform, reduction in taxes, an end to useless offices and unearned pensions, repeal of the corn laws (this from a farmer ! ! !), the abolition of slavery, and in very heavy type, the Total Abolition of Tithes. After that outburst Juxon seems to have shot his bolt, and there is no evidence of further meetings of the Aldridge Political Union. The next year Juxon began his campaign for educational reform.

Political Reform was often associated with Trade Unions and Trade Unions were often disguised as Friendly Societies. Nevertheless the Aldridge Friendly Society seems to have been genuine and not associated with Juxon or the Political Union. It started in 1817 to help the sick, ensure decent burials, and, one suspects, for the joys of an occasional social evening. The members met at the sign of the Anchor every fourth Saturday, winter six p.m. to nine p.m., summer seven p.m. to ten p.m. The subscription was one shilling and two-pence per member every club night. Two members served as constables bringing in the beer as required (and if they brought any excess they had to pay for the excess out of their own pockets). Funds were kept in a box with three locks, the keys being held by different people. Swearing or betting could be punished by a fine of twopence and there was a much more severe fine for fighting. Members had to be elected. The benefits offered included £2 to £3 to cover a wife's funeral, and £5 to £8 for a member's funeral. Sick pay was seven shillings per week and there was a scheme of visiting to prevent malingering. Balloting was by black and white beans. On June 24th each year the Society held its annual feast, when all had to pay eighteenpence for food and sixpence for ale. The members met on that day at ten a.m. 'in decent clothes' and proceeded to church, where they listened to a sermon, for which they paid one guinea. The feast followed the sermon.

There were probably Political Unionists at Great Barr as well as at Aldridge, for General Dyott during 1832 entered in his diary:

On June 1st I attended a Petty Sessions at Barr on the request of Mr. Leigh who was unable to be present on account of indisposition. The chief business was occasioned by numerous informations for not having the name of owner of carts and waggons in the proper place on the carriage. One of the great orators of the Birmingham Political Union appeared as advocate for the proprietor of a beer shop on a charge of having his house open at improper hours. Notwithstanding the pleading of the great reformer (Mr. Edmonds), he was convicted.

Meanwhile, the lord of Great Barr, Sir Edward Dolman Scott, was also indulging in politics, the following being another extract from the General's diary and is dated 1830:

On the 24th I went to Barr to dine and sleep for the purpose of attending Sir Edward Scott's publick entry to Lichfield to a dinner given by the True Blue Club. A grand procession took place accordingly the next day. We left Barr about ten o'clock to arrive at the canal bridge near Lichfield before twelve. Sir Edward, Mr. The. Levett, Mr. Burnes Floyer and myself in an open carriage belonging to the former. The horses were immediately taken off, and twentyfour free-men in blue jackets and blue ropes were attached to the carriage, and drew us into town and through the principal streets to the Swan Inn, accompanied by the largest collection of persons I ever saw assembled at Lichfield. Triumphal arches were formed in various parts with applicable mottoes and also abundance of blue flags of all descriptions. Nearly five hundred dined ; a most abundant supply was provided ; Sir Edward Scott, Sir Roger Gresley, Sir George Chetwynd, and Mr. Levett (Recorder) each sent a buck. A fine jollification of punch and ale with shouting and singing to make the welkin roar.

The General often visited Sir Edward Scott (son of Sir Joseph Scott) and on one occasion described him as 'a good humoured country gentleman but possessing none of the wit and humour of his father'. When he wrote that, the General was in a good humour himself, having just taken part in a day's shooting at Barr which yielded a bag of fifty-eight pheasants, fourteen hares, six rabbits, one woodcock and one partridge.

BIBLIOGRAPHY

Charity Commissioners, Report 1825, Vol. X.

Aris's Birmingham Gazette.

Finch Smith, *Notes and Collections of the Parish of Aldridge.*

B.R.L. Broadsheet Aldridge Political Union, Aug. 1832.
Broadsheet Aldridge Political Council, Sept. 1832.
Broadsheet Aldridge Free Grammar School, Feb. 1833.

Juxon, Pamphlet, *To the Public and Inhabitants of Aldridge*, Apl. 1833.
Pamphlet, *To the Inhabitants of Aldridge*, July, 1844.

B.R.L., Prospectus of Druid-Heath School.

Rules of Aldridge Free Grammar School, 1829 (in possession of Mr. Partridge, Clerk to the Governors of the Cooper Jordan Endowed School).

Wm. Salt Library, Prospectus of Aldridge School under the direction of Mr. and Mrs. Allport and Miss Gray.

C.R.O., Rules of Aldridge Friendly Society.

Jeffery, Dyotts Diary.

CHAPTER XII

TRANSPORT AND INDUSTRY

IN TUDOR TIMES the central government had placed the responsibility for maintaining the roads on the parish. Each year the parish appointed one or more 'Surveyors' to superintend the work on the roads, the poorer people working unpaid for six days each year as directed by the 'Surveyor', whilst the richer people had to supply a man, horse and cart, for six days. The Surveyor, since he usually held office for one year only, knew little of road building or maintenance, whilst the unpaid workers, probably did as little as they could without getting into trouble. It was possible to pay (compound) instead of working unpaid, and a number of villagers did this, but in any case, supplementary paid labour had to be hired, and materials bought. To meet the cost of this, special rates were levied as needed and detailed accounts were kept.

'Ale, Bread & Cheese' figures largely in these accounts, being apparently supplied to all labourers. During June, 1773, the month that year in which most of the work was done on the roads, Great Barr spent forty-three shillings and threepence on these items; the paid labourers at that time receiving only eighteenpence per day. The method of repair appears to have been to break up the road, sometimes with a plough, level it and add gravel and stones. The gravel was obtained from the common, or after the enclosures, from the gravel pits which the Enclosure Commissioners had provided. The Aldridge gravel pit was in front of Coppy Hall, where there is now a pool, whilst one of the Great Barr pits is now represented by the triangle where Longwood Road meets Barr Common Road, the pit having recently been filled in and grassed over. Stones were bought by the cartload from local farmers who presumably had them picked from their fields. Marshy land was a problem, but one solution attempted was to float the road over small bogs on bundles of ling (kids). The following entries taken from the Great Barr accounts are typical:

1776 Pd for 15 Hundred ling kids at 3/- per hundred.....................£2 6s. 6d.
Pd for 57 loads of stones at 4d. per load.......................................19s. od.
Pd for mending ye tools..3s. 3d.
Pd 6 labourers ....9s. od.
Pd for suff bricks (i.e. for drainage)..3s. od.
Pd for throwing up ye Jourdans lane...................................£3 6s. od.

The history of the gravel pit outside Coppy Hall, although a trivial matter in itself, serves to show how parish affairs were sometimes conducted, despite the watch-dog activities of Charles Juxon. The pit was provided for the parish during the enclosures between 1795 and 1799, at which time Coppy Hall was being used as a school, first by Rev. James Lomax and later by the Rev. William Cowley. Coppy Hall later passed to the Rev. Davids. This gentleman had been curate of Great Barr but had married the rich widow of Mr. Hawkesford, who had lived at 'The Chestnuts', a large house which stood at the foot of High Street, where the Elms public house now stands. The Rev. Davids was a trustee of the 'Free Grammar School'. He left Aldridge but wished to buy the gravel pit, presumably to increase the value of Coppy Hall. On August 25th, 1839 he wrote to Mr. Jackson, then Schoolmaster, who was serving that year as Surveyor. The Rev. Davids pointed out that a small piece of land near the Great Barr Gravel Pit was up for sale, if he bought the land would the parish accept it in exchange for the pit at Coppy Hall, and if so would Mr. Jackson attend the auction and buy the land on his behalf. Jackson did buy it for £59, but the exchange was held up because Mr. Lea, a rich and powerful parishioner, who had business interests in Birmingham, objected. He contended that his tenants had a right to water their cattle at the Coppy Hall pit and produced a legal opinion supporting this. Jackson meanwhile applied to the Quarter Sessions, who consented that as the parish might more conveniently obtain gravel from the land of Mr. Jackson, than elsewhere, the parish might buy gravel from him. This cut out the need for the Coppy Hall pit and gravel began to be drawn from the land purchased for the Rev. Davids, Jackson making a charge for the gravel. This pit can still be seen on Barr Common Road, partly filled in, and opposite the junction with Longwood Road. The Quarter Sessions next refused to allow the parish to sell the Coppy Hall pit to Davids and build a well for Mr. Lea's tenants, but the Quarter Sessions stated they would agree, if Rev. Davids built the well. Jackson consequently arranged with Rev. Davids to reduce the valuation of the gravel pit at Coppy Hall from £80 to £70 and to use the £10 thus cheated from the parish to build the well. This was done, but in February, 1840 the Rev. Davids was writing to Jackson to ensure that the transaction was completed before the end of Jackson's turn of office as Surveyor. If the enclosure award be examined it will be seen that the award has at some date been altered to provide for the provision of the well and for the maintenance of it out of parish funds. One wonders when the alteration was made and why.

The most important road at Aldridge was the Chester Road, which was one of the roads that linked London with Chester, at that time the port of embarkation for Ireland, Holyhead being almost inaccessible. This road would be little used by the parishioners, who probably considered the roads in the centre of the village to be more important. Hence it is not surprising that the road was often in a bad state of repair. Prior to the enclosures it ran across Barr Common and Aldridge Common without fence or hedge on either side.

John Wesley, travelling from Birmingham, wrote in his Journal on February 20th, 1746:

> We set out before it was light. Before we came to Aldridge Heath, the rain changed into snow which the northerly winds drove full in our faces, and crusted us over from head to foot in less than an hour's time. We inquired of one who lived at the entrance of the moors, which was the best way to Stafford. " Sir " said he ' 'Tis a thousand pounds to a penny that you do not come there today. Why 'tis four long miles to the far side of the common and on a clear day I am not sure to go right across it, and now all the roads are covered with snow and it snows so that you cannot see before you." However we went on, and I believe did not get ten yards out of the way till we came to Stafford.

The route Wesley followed is not certain. He may have travelled along the Chester Road or he may have passed over Barr Common, into Aldridge and then over Druid Heath and Aldridge Common.

During the eighteenth century the Chester Road was carrying much important traffic despite the more popular alternative route from London, which branched off at Castle Bromwich and reached Chester by way of Lichfield and Stone. In addition to the Chester coaches, there were coaches to Shrewsbury and beyond. The roads were bad and the coaches slow. In 1739 the Chester coach took six days to reach London. Drawn by six and sometimes eight horses, it travelled from dawn to dusk, the passengers sleeping at inns at Whitchurch, Stonnall, Coventry, Northampton and Dunstable. One can sympathise with the passengers cooped up in a small uncomfortable coach together for six days of discomfort.

Swift wrote of the journey to Chester:

Rous'd from sound sleep—thrice called—at length I rise
Yawning, stretch out my arm, half closed my eyes ;
By steps and lanthorn enter the machine,
And take my place—how cordially—between
Two aged matrons of excessive bulk,
To mend the matter, too, of meaner folk ;
While in like mood, jamm'd in on t'other side,
A bullying captain and a fair one ride,
Foolish as fair, and in her lap a boy—
Our plague eternal, but her only joy.
At last, the glorious number to complete,
Steps in my landlord for that bodkin seat ;
When soon by every hillock, rut and stone,
Into each other's face by turn we're thrown.
This grandam scolds, that coughs, the captain swears,
The fair one screams and has a thousand fears ;
While our plump landlord, train'd in other lore,
Slumbers at ease, nor yet asham'd to snore ;
And Master Dicky, in his mother's lap,
Squalling, at once brings up three meals of pap.
Sweet company ! Next time I do protest Sir,
I'd walk to Dublin, ere I'd ride to Chester.

In addition to the discomfort, there was the danger of highway robbery. In 1703 the Shrewsbury coach was robbed by a gang at Brownhills and later six men and three women were charged with the offence, but not before they had committed other robberies with violence on the road. In 1751 the 'Shrewsbury Caravan' was held up in the same district and robbed by a highwayman who stated that he was a distressed tradesman and courteously passed round his hat, taking up a forced collection, but refusing to accept coppers.

The coaches that stayed in Stonnall put up at the Welsh Harp, which stood in Stonnall beside the Swan, which was opened in opposition. It should not be confused with the Irish Harp. Sanders, in his *History of Shenstone*, has told the story of the rise and fall of this inn.

In addition to the stage coaches were the goods wagons. The Wakemans were Aldridge farmers and were also carriers running three wagons weekly to both London and Chester. These wagons often carried passengers who could not afford the fare needed to travel on the ordinary coach. The wagons travelling between the two towns made Aldridge one of the places where they stayed the night, the London wagon leaving the Chester Road and travelling to Aldridge over Barr Common, though fresh horses were often needed to help it over the spur of Barr Beacon. The Wakemans had stabling in High Street and one can imagine that the travellers were welcomed for any news they carried. It was said that when the wagon from Chester arrived on the same night as the wagon from London, Aldridge was crowded.

From about 1750, traffic along the Aldridge portion of the Chester Road steadily declined, as coaches turned to new routes following better roads and passing through more centres of population where passengers could be picked up or set down. The route through Birmingham and Walsall became increasingly popular. By 1780 coaches were running to Holyhead as well as to Chester; by 1802 it is said that only the Liverpool Mail passed through Stonnall and Aldridge.

The diversion of the stage coaches was mainly due to the improvement of the Walsall roads by turnpiking. The first Walsall Act had been obtained in 1748, but it was following the Act of 1766 that the big change was made. The road between Walsall and Wyrley was improved, and Ablewell Street constructed so that the coaches need not pass along steep and narrow Birmingham Street and High Street. Walsall then became a coaching centre; the coaches travelling between Walsall and Birmingham by way of Great Barr. These coaches included the 'Royal Mails' to London, Bristol, Manchester, Wolverhampton and Leeds; the 'Aurora' (Liverpool and London); the 'Despatch' (Chester and London); the 'Magnet' (Liverpool and London); the 'Tally Ho' (to Birmingham), and a post coach to Nottingham. Speeds increased and the coaches were very different from the slow coaches that had crawled across Aldridge Heath. Telford's work on the Holyhead Road caused a further diversion, the coaches then travelling between Birmingham and Wolverhampton via Wednesbury. Then coaches were able to reach Holyhead from London in just over a full day's travelling.

Some attempt was made to improve the Chester Road and the branch from it to Birmingham by way of Saltley. In 1759 an Act was passed for the turnpiking of the whole route from Chester to Castle Bromwich. This long stretch was divided into four sections, the fourth section being from the Welsh Harp to Castle Bromwich. This section was to be controlled by trustees, one hundred and sixty-eight in number, plus the mayor and corporation of Coventry. The trustees named included J. B. Hawkesford of Aldridge and Thomas Hoo of Great Barr. Despite the large number of trustees, the 1759 Act fixed the quorum at only seven; in 1777 this was reduced to five, and in 1801 to only three. So much for the interest that they took. The tolls collected at the tollgate erected by the Welsh Harp, included threepence for a horse and cart, one penny for a packhorse or mule, tenpence for a score of cattle, and fivepence for a score of pigs or sheep. The parishioners were expected to do part of their statutory six days unpaid labour on the Chester Road but Aldridge soon compounded for £30 per annum and Great Barr for £12 per annum. A glance at a map will show that traffic from the north (especially drovers with livestock for the growing Birmingham market, who would prefer to pass over commons where their animals could freely feed) could easily by-pass the Turnpike Gate at the Welsh Harp, by leaving the Chester Road and travelling through Pelsall, Rushall and Barr Common; or through Walsall Wood, Aldridge and Barr Common. The traffic could then either rejoin the Chester Road near the Parson & Clerk Inn, or else travel on to Birmingham by way of Perry Barr. No wonder the fourth section was unprofitable. An Act of 1777 was principally concerned with preventing traffic from the south by-passing the Saltley Gate, but it also refers to a common local practice of avoiding payment of tolls. A vehicle normally only paid tolls once per day, no matter how frequently it passed through the turnpike. The Act states:

> . . . whereas it is become the practice for persons to draw or carry Iron, Ironstone, Lead, Coals, Wood, Goods, and things on Carriages to near the Turnpike Gate or Bars, and there to unload or lay down the same in large quantities, and upon a future day to draw or carry the same away through the Turnpike Gate or Bar without being subject to paying the Toll more than once for passing several times through the Gate or Bar.

Hence the Act forbade goods to be laid down within five hundred yards of a tollgate or within thirty yards of the centre of the road: penalty for first offence twenty shillings, second offence forty shillings.

As the fourth section still continued unprofitable tolls were raised by another Act (1787). Coaches with three or more horses then were charged eighteenpence, whilst those with two horses escaped for ninepence. Further Acts followed in 1801 and 1823, but the section never paid its way; by-passing was too easy and the new roads through Walsall or Wednesbury too attractive. During twenty-eight weeks of 1824 the gate at Stonnall yielded only £48 13s. 2½d. in tolls.

The road passing from Lichfield to Walsall through Rushall was also turnpiked, with a gate near the end of Cartbridge Lane and a bar at Station Street, then known as Coal Pool Lane.

Despite the improvement in the roads, the carriage of goods was still expensive, as can be seen from the details given earlier of the cost of carriage of church bells between Great Barr and Leicester. Throughout the eighteenth century there had been many proposals put forward for the building of a canal in this district, but not until the end of the century was one actually built. In 1792 an Act was obtained for building the Wyrley and Essington Canal. This joined the Birmingham and Wolverhampton Canal at Wolverhampton, and the Coventry Canal (and so gave access to the Trent and Mersey Canal) at Huddlesford, north of Lichfield. It was built mainly to secure the coal traffic from pits in the Pelsall and Wyrley area. A branch was added from Catshill through Walsall Wood to the limestone quarries at Rushall and Hays Head. A feature of the canal was that boats could follow a circuitous route of some twenty miles from Hays Head to Wolverhampton by way of Rushall, Catshill, Pelsall and Wednesfield, without encountering a single lock until the flight at Wolverhampton was reached. Not until 1840 was the canal extended from Longwood to give easy access to Birmingham. Near the Longwood locks can still be seen the disused portion of the canal running off towards Hays Head.

This canal brought a new lease of life to the lime industry, giving easy access to most parts of the Midlands. It also helped the development of the brickworks and later the coalmines in the Stubbers Green and Leighswood areas.

The first railways were built here some fifty years after the canal. In 1837 the Grand Junction Railway (later L. & N.W.R.) was opened linking Wolverhampton with Birmingham via Bescot and with a station at Hamstead, named Great Barr. In 1846 two schemes for new railways were amalgamated. One scheme was for a railway from Dudley to Walsall, and the other for a line from Bescot to Walsall and on to join the Birmingham and Derby Railway (later Midland Railway) at Wichnor, with stations at Rushall, Pelsall, and Lichfield. The joint schemes were given the title 'South Staffordshire Railway'.

The Walsall-Bescot portion of the railway was opened in 1847, the L.N.W.R. running trains for the new company from Walsall to Bescot and then on over their own lines to Birmingham. The Walsall-Wichnor portion opened in 1849 with the stations at Rushall and Pelsall, as planned; the company then also began to use its own rolling stock and locomotives. In 1850, the company foolishly came to an agreement with its manager, for him to maintain the rolling stock and run the trains, without realising that they were giving him power to run trains as and when he pleased—in fact, giving him complete control over the whole concern. They found it a very costly business extricating themselves from that agreement. The L.N.W.R. then ran the trains for the South Staffordshire Company; a far from satisfactory arrangement, as was shown at the inquiry into an accident which happened on December 23rd, 1854.

A goods train with two engines travelling towards Walsall was delayed shunting at Pelsall Colliery. Neither of the two drivers had previously driven over the line and the firemen also were unacquainted with it. The drivers, who had previously had an argument as to which engine should head the train, were not pleased at being delayed. Whilst shunting, a second train approached, and to the drivers' further annoyance, passed on to Pelsall in front of them. Eventually the first train left the colliery and set off in pursuit, only to be stopped at Pelsall Station and told to draw into a siding to allow a passenger train to pass. The drivers refused and blocked both lines with their train, but when they stated that they were almost out of water, they were allowed to proceed in front of the passenger train. The drivers set off again at a furious speed, a signalman remarking, 'Them gentlemen means going it'. The train had to pass two level crossings—Hombridge and Ryecroft; at neither was there a fixed signal. The first crossing was controlled by a married woman and the second by a girl of thirteen, both however exhibited the correct signals by means of flags, but the train tore on to collide with the second train which was halted outside Walsall station. One fireman was killed. The average speed of the first train from the time of leaving the colliery until the time of the collision, despite the delay at Pelsall station was thirty m.p.h., according to the Inspecting Officer who investigated and reported on the accident. The L.N.W.R. stated that part of the trouble was the excessive hours worked by their men and engines when operating trains for the South Staffordshire Railway, the men being then beyond the control of the L.N.W.R. On December 18th previous to the accident one engine and crew had been continuously on duty for twenty-three hours, whilst the same engine had also been on duty on December 19th, 20th, 21st and 22nd for fourteen, nineteen, fifteen and nineteen hours respectively. On one occasion since the crash an engine and crew had been continuously on duty for a spell of twenty-six hours ten minutes.

Eventually, the L.N.W.R. took over the whole railway and in 1861 claimed running powers, which the Midland Company denied, from Wichnor into Burton. The L.N.W.R. then advised the Midland that they were going to send a train along the Rushall-Pelsall branch through Wichnor to Burton. This was duly sent with the L.N.W.R. District Superintendent on board, only to find at Wichnor, the Midland Superintendent, a large body of platelayers and two or three engines in steam, one of which blocked the path, being chained to the crossing. Inquiry showed that the Midland had heard that the L.N.W.R. train was carrying three hundred men to help force the first entry into Burton and to establish the right for L.N.W.R. trains to run there. Both superintendents telegraphed for instructions and eventually the Midland gave way, the L.N.W.R. engine being allowed to enter Burton 'blowing triumphant cock crows on its whistle'.

The branch line of the Midland Railway, built through Aldridge to link Castle Bromwich with Walsall and with a connection to Wolverhampton via North Walsall, was opened for goods traffic on May 19th, 1879. On July 1st of the same year the first passenger services were run from Birmingham New Street to Streetly for the race meeting held there in the Park. The journey took thirty-five minutes and the third-class single fare was eightpence-halfpenny. It has been said that the Midland Company did not know what name to give the station at Streetly, there being no village there then; and that the station was nearly called Jervistown in honour of the Hon. Parker Jervis who resided at Little Aston Hall, who disliked the idea of the station bearing that name. However this may be, when the first train ran, the station was named 'Streetly'.

The branch line from Aldridge to Walsall Wood and the various collieries was opened on July 1st, 1884. The line was intended for mineral traffic but some trains were run (never more than three per day) for passengers between Aldridge, Walsall Wood and Brownhills (Midland). Mostly, the passengers were miners travelling to and from work. The passenger train service was withdrawn on March 29th, 1930, and part of the double track has since been removed so that the branch is in effect a single line used only for traffic from the collieries and brickyards, and for wagon storage.

The coming of the canals and railways and the use of steam in industry enabled the district to take advantage of the natural resources here. Before the cutting of the canal, this had only been attempted in a small way. The limestone quarries which had existed since the Middle Ages were almost derelict, and the mines and brickyard were small. The plan drawn for the proposed extension of the Wyrley and Essington Canal to Hays Head (1793) shows a small brick-kiln near the present works of the Aldridge Brick, Tile & Coal Company, 'old Coal Pits' to the west of Dumblederry Lane, four lime works at Daw End, Linley and Hays Head, and a colliery at Pelsall. Limestone quarries by Moss Close, then part of Rushall, came back into use after lying idle for many years, a steam engine being used to keep the workings clear of water. Part of the limestone at Rushall was quarried and part was mined, using steampower for haulage and pumping. Some shafts were between two and three hundred feet deep, being driven to reach a seam of limestone eleven yards thick. There were, of course, smaller seams. In one case the workings were approached by an inclined tunnel and there donkey haulage is reputed to have been used. At Hays Head all the limestone was quarried, and was reputed to be of very high quality, very suitable for the making of cement. In 1813 lime was selling at four shillings and threepence per quarter and demand was reputed to be much in excess of supply. In 1856 Glew wrote his *History of the Borough and Foreign of Walsall* and described the works at Linley, referring to 'caverns of immense extent which lead to a large subterranean lake . . . they are visited in the summers seasons by numerous pleasure parties, when they are sometimes brilliantly illuminated, producing a fairy scene of extraordinary splendour'.

By 1851 brickmaking had expanded so that the blue brick works of Brawn & Arrowsmith, off the Walsall Wood Road (now Joberns Ltd.) employed two hundred hands and two steam engines. The collieries continued to develop at Pelsall, where there was also an iron works and a firm of 'Millwrights, Engineers and Boilermakers'. Nevertheless, a number of nailers still persisted, particularly at Pelsall, working at their ancient but depressed, typically Black Country, craft.

BIBLIOGRAPHY

C.R.O., Aldridge Parish Documents.

Great Barr Parish Chest.   Surveyors' Accounts.

J. Wesley, *Journal*.

Sanders, *History of Shenstone*.

Hackwood, *Chronicles of Cannock Chase*.

Harper, *The Holyhead Road*.

Stretton, *History of the Midland Railway*.

Robinson, South Staffordshire Railway and its Locomotives (*Railway Magazine*, Sept. 1935).

Piggot, *National and Commercial Directory*, 1828.

B.R.L.   Pitt, A plan of the proposed extession to the Wyrley and Essington Canal.

B.R.L.   Inspecting Officer of Railways, Report upon an accident on the South Staffordshire Railway, Dec. 23rd, 1854.

White, *History, Gazeteer and Directory of Staffordshire*, 1834, 1851.

Acts of Parliament (B.R.L. 16997)—

    33 George II, Cap. 51.

    18 George III, Cap. 86.

    28 George III, Cap. 107.

    42 George III, Cap. 81.

     4 George IV, Cap. 121.

CHAPTER XIII

THE LAST HUNDRED YEARS

THE LAST CENTURY has seen tremendous changes, far greater even than those caused by the enclosures. These changes have necessarily been accompanied and partly made possible by big changes in local administration. The enclosures killed the Manor Court, which had already lost much authority to the secular Parish with its vestry of ratepayers. After 1834 the secular parish also declined, for in that year the Poor Law Act was passed which, for Poor Law purposes joined the parishes into Unions controlled by Guardians elected by a plural voting system based on property qualifications. Aldridge, Great Barr, Rushall and Pelsall, together with Bentley, Darlaston and the Borough and Foreign of Walsall were placed in the Walsall Union which had a central workhouse at Pleck Road, Walsall. The Walsall Rural Sanitary District, which included all the present Urban District, was set up in 1881, the Staffordshire County Council was formed in 1888, and the Walsall Rural District Council in 1894. This latter controlled Bentley, Aldridge, Great Barr, Rushall and Pelsall, each of which had their own separate Parish Councils.

The outstanding figure on the Rural District Council was the chairman, bluff Joseph Clare, who for long lived on Longwood Road. He was engaged in the manufacture of leather goods at Walsall and had lost his right arm in an accident with a machine used to split hides. It is said that within a month he was back at work, and despite having only a left arm, had mastered the machine. Later he became a very active Justice of the Peace, who despite his forthright manner, showed a personal concern to help some of the unfortunates brought before him. The Rural District Council had need of a strong chairman such as he, for there was some feeling between the parishes. Most of the Council's time was spent on such matters as sewers, drainage and street lighting and some progress was made.

Earlier the water supply had caused the Rural Sanitary Authority some concern. In 1884 the Medical Officer reported that:

The South Staffordshire Waterworks Company during the last few months have brought their mains to Aldridge. Several houses in the village have been and others are being connected. They have also extended the mains on the Beacon side of Great Barr and three cottages there have had water laid on. The water supply at Ten House Row has been improved, the pump having been taken up and the well cleansed. The same has been done in Pig Lane in connection with a pump and well supplying fifteen houses. At Pelsall eighty seven houses have been furnished with the Company's water.

Nine years later the Medical Officer again reported:

Respecting the water supply at Great Barr referred to in my last report, it will be remembered that a canvas of property owners was ordered with a view to obtain their consent to take the Company's water in the event of the mains being extended to that place. Particulars were obtained and it was found that the whole of the property on the route belonged to one proprietor whose agent I regret to say declined to recommend it. Consequently nothing further has been done in the matter.

Walsall has several times cast envious eyes on the area, and in 1920 the Borough made an attempt to swallow the Rural District wholesale. One of the main contentions was lack of facilities in the Rural District. Earlier, in 1876 and 1890, Walsall boundaries had been pushed forward into Rushall, taking in the Butts, Ryecroft and Calderfields. This time the bid failed, although some Rushall councillors wished all Rushall to become part of Walsall. Besides pointing to lack of facilities Walsall claimed that some of what facilities there were, were already provided by Walsall, especially Transport and Gas. At one time Aldridge had had its own Gas Works but some years previously these works which were at Leighswood, had been purchased and absorbed by the Walsall Corporation.

In 1934 the Aldridge Urban District was set up composed of the same parishes as the Rural District save for Bentley, which was then excluded. The development of Aldridge followed rapidly. In 1933 there had only been half-a-dozen houses in Anchor Lane; but by 1940 Anchor Road was the centre of the village, with the new Council House, Police Station, Police Court, Cinema, Methodist Church and a number of shops.

Aldridge is fortunate in having a lofty, extensive park—Barr Beacon—which can be freely used. It has been claimed that fifteen counties are visible from the summit. As stated earlier, the hill may well have been used as a beacon in Tudor times, certainly it was equipped as a beacon during the Napoleonic period. Since then, on festive occasions, such as Queen Victoria's Jubilee, huge bonfires have been made there. In 1918 Colonel Wilkinson gave the summit as a memorial to those Warwickshire and Staffordshire men who fell in the First World War. It is controlled by a joint committee representing the surrounding local authorities, with Aldridge U.D.C. acting as the executive authority.

The Lord of the Manor has long ceased to wield much influence in Aldridge, despite the building some time prior to 1851 of the large manor house at the end of High Street by Edward Tongue, the successor to the Croxalls. At Great Barr, Sir Francis Edward Scott succeeded the 'True Blue' Sir Edward, but unfortunately Sir Francis died in 1863 at the early age of thirty-nine. He had spent much time abroad, especially in Italy, for he was keenly interested in art and was one of the pillars of the Birmingham Midland Institute. He did much by personal service and gifts to forward art and culture generally in that city. His widow, Lady Scott, continued to reside at Great Barr Hall, but had little influence on the neighbourhood though she obtained some notoriety when, in 1890, six children were prosecuted for damaging the undergrowth at Great Barr Hall to the value of sixpence, whilst gathering bluebells. In 1911 the Hall and grounds were taken over by the Walsall and West Bromwich Guardians as a home for the progressive treatment of the mentally defective. The era of the Scotts was over. Great Barr Hall, on which Sir Joseph lavished so much money, is now St. Margaret's Hospital, administered by the Regional Hospital Board.

During the century the once flourishing limestone mines and quarries have again declined and all are now closed. In 1902 two companies were still mining stone, the Daw End Works, employing seventeen men underground and fourteen on the surface, whilst J. Brawn's Phoenix Works had ten underground and six on the surface. Later, Lavender Limited opened another works, but that was short-lived and was closed in April, 1911. The East Anglian Cement Company was by then operating the Linley Works. During the first World War only the Phoenix Works remained open, and they were closed in July, 1918. The Linley Works, however, re-opened again soon afterwards, but production was on a small scale. In 1938, only eight men were employed there. Production was again stopped during the Second World War, when the R.A.F. used the caverns for bomb storage. A recent attempt to re-open the works has finally been abandoned because of alterations made by the R.A.F. and flooding.

Brickmaking has continued to expand. The firms are all concentrated in a small area between Leighswood and Walsall Wood. The coalmines were also in the same district, which was described in the report 'Birmingham and its Regional Setting', prepared for the 1950 meeting of the British Association in Birmingham, as 'more extensively disfigured, perhaps, than any area of comparable size in the Black Country'. It is a mixture of swags (pools caused by subsidence), derelict pit mounds, clay quarries and brickworks and would be completely unrecognisable to anyone who only knew the district as it was a hundred years ago.

It is uncertain when the coalmines were first opened, but by 1881 the Leighswood Colliery had not only opened but had also failed, throwing many out of work, and according to Finch Smith, was the cause of some thirty cottages at Leighswood being vacant. There had been trouble at the colliery for some time. The previous year some employees had been summoned for failing to work, but the case against them was dismissed. The men apparently had withheld their labour when they feared they would be working for a contractor and not directly for the Colliery Company; a previous contractor had failed to pay wages in full.

There were a number of fatal accidents at the collieries, but usually the number of victims was small, as in 1859 at Pelsall Wood Colliery when the winding machinery was working out of gear; or in 1876, when a hanging scaffold used in a shaft at the Leighswood Colliery fell three hundred yards with two men on it. In 1871, at Highbridge Colliery, Pelsall, a shallow seam below saturated sand and gravel was being worked when the roof collapsed and sand and water rushed in causing three deaths.

The accident at Pelsall Hall Colliery in 1872 was a major one On Thursday morning, November 14th, the night shift came off duty and all seemed well as the day shift took over. At breakfast time some of the day shift came out of the pit, and as they sat on the bank they were alarmed by the urgent cry 'Pull up' from the bottom of the shaft. The 'bonnet' was immediately pulled up with three men clinging to it. A skip was then quickly lowered to the men and boys who could be heard as they swam at the bottom of the shaft in rapidly rising water. Eight were rescued on the skip, which was again lowered, but this time fruitlessly. Apart from the noise of rushing water, all was silent at the pit bottom. Twenty-two men were known to be still underground and the rapidly spreading news brought crowds of anxious relatives and friends to the pit bank. Everything possible was done to pump out the water, but the pit could not be cleared for several days, and when at last it was possible to descend to the workings, rescue operations were hampered by choke damp. It seems that the miners had struck some old flooded workings whose existence had not been suspected, and hence the rush of water flooding the pit. All twenty-two of the trapped men died. Visitors to the scene of the disaster included Sister Dora (when there was still hope that some of the victims might be brought up alive) and Bishop Selwyn of Lichfield. The latter is justly famous for his exploits as the first Bishop of New Zealand, and his ready sympathy on this occasion seems to have endeared him to the mining community.

Despite the accidents, mining soon became the major industry. In 1889, the Aldridge Colliery Company were working their No. 1 and No. 2 Pits, whilst Edward Barnett of Coppy Hall ran the Coppy Hall Colliery at Stubbers Green. These are all described in the official list of mines as working both ironstone and coal—a common practice in South Staffordshire. At Pelsall were Fishley Colliery (No. 1), Pelsall Colliery, Pelsall Hall Colliery and Hope Colliery. Two years later Pelsall Wood Colliery appeared on the list of mines. The size of the industry can be seen from the following figures:

	Colliery			Underground workers	Surface workers
1902	Aldridge No. 1	...	...	462	183
	No. 2	...	...	489	122
	Coppy Hall	...	...	240	74
	Pelsall	...	...	...	184	90
1906	Aldridge No. 1	...	...	542	175
	No. 2	...	...	620	143
	Coppy Hall	...	...	258	83
	Pelsall Grove	...	...	12	4
1933	Aldridge No. 1	...	...	777	238
1936	Aldridge No. 1	...	...	453	163

The Coppy Hall Colliery was abandoned during August, 1909; Aldridge No. 2 followed on the last day of December, 1930, and finally Aldridge No. 1 was also closed in October, 1936. The importance of the industry can be seen when it is remembered that the Aldridge and Pelsall Collieries employed a total of 1,837 men in 1906, and yet the total population, men, women and children, resident in the parishes of Aldridge and Pelsall in 1911 was only 6,303. Up to the early 1930's the streets of Aldridge were crowded at different times during the day as miners tramped to work carrying their wicker 'snap' boxes, or else returned, tired and grimy, for it was before the era of pithead baths. The choice of employment before Aldridge boys was small. It was the pits for the majority and agriculture for a few, or perhaps brickmaking. Travel out of Aldridge to work was difficult, there was no 'bus service to Walsall before 1920.

Apart from the closing down of the local pits, mining was depressed between the wars, with often many men working short weeks. The unrest culminated in the General Strike of 1926, when all public transport as well as mining ceased and those who wished to travel to Walsall went on foot or by cycle. Miner's children went to school armed with dinner plates and at mid-day scurried off to the Red Lion for a free meal.

It would have been understandable if with the depression of mining and the closing of the local pits, the size of the population had steadily shrunk. Instead, the figures show a remarkable increase.

Census figures are complicated by the change from the Rural District to the Urban District with its slightly different boundary and wards, but the population of the area represented by the present Urban District appears to have been as follows:

1921 ...	...	...	11,978
1931 ...	...	...	14,446
1939 ...	...	...	20,420
1951 ...	...	...	29,171
June, 1956	...	...	35,930

An analysis of the 1951 figures shows that at that date most of the increase was caused by the arrival of families with parents in the thirty to forty-five age range and with children under the age of ten. It is planned that the population shall continue to expand until it reaches 55,000.

The expansion of population is not due to the arrival here of new industries. As late as 1956 few of the new factories were in full production. The expansion is due rather to the proximity of the heavily overcrowded conurbation of Birmingham and the Black Country, together with vastly improved transport facilities made possible by the internal combustion engine and the resulting 'bus services which, with private cars, make it only too easy to live in Aldridge and work in industrial Birmingham or Walsall. Since the collapse of mining there has been a real danger that Aldridge would become a mere dormitory. Between that collapse and the Second World War almost the only industries in Aldridge were brick-making, engineering (carried on by several small firms) and plastic moulding. The latter industry was carried on at 'Streetly Works', which was a munition factory during the First World War, later used for the manufacture of detonators for use on railways (fog signals) and finally devoted to the making of small plastic articles. Most Aldridge people had to travel outside Aldridge for their daily work.

Prior to 1920, travel to Walsall or Birmingham meant travel by train, cycle or, as was often the case, on foot. For a brief period about the turn of the century, there had been a horse 'bus service to Walsall on market days. Rushall residents were fortunate, being able to use the tramcar service which ran from Walsall to Walsall

Wood. This service, which was commenced in 1904, led to the closing of the railway station at Rushall. The tramcars were withdrawn in 1928. On July 27th, 1920, the Walsall Corporation began the first motor 'bus service to Aldridge (route No. 6). Since then the 'bus services have developed, making the dormitory danger possible.

Whether that danger is successfully weathered or not still remains to be seen. The U.D.C., alert to the danger, have set aside a big stretch of poor farming land reaching from the Red House Estate to Daw End for industrial development. New factories are shooting up there. Some works, such as that of the B.R.D., which employs about one thousand workers, represent new industries, the B.R.D. being engaged in the making of turbine blades for gas turbines. Others, such as McKechnie Brothers, makers of brass extrusions, whose works will eventually employ over a thousand workers, represent firms moving to Aldridge from congested areas, especially Birmingham. The largest factory so far planned (January, 1957) is that of Birlec Limited, which will occupy some thirty-four acres. The building of this has not yet commenced.

There has been little provision for social activities and recreation until recently. When the annual bull-baiting at Rushall ended about 1830 for long there remained but cock-fighting (soon made illegal) and the wakes. The latter degenerated into visits by gaudy fairs presented by travelling showmen. Even the arrival of these was looked forward to, and as September 14th approached Aldridge children looked anxiously for the coming of 'the big engine' with its string of vans. Early in this century the local schools celebrated with a halfday holiday when 'Gaffer Stephens' and his staff patronised the wake. About 1880, the Vicar of Rushall, Rev. F. G. Littlecot, acquired the Three Horse Shoes public house, which had become notorious. He closed it down and extinguished the license. An attempt to use the premises as a shop failed, and later it was converted to a 'Coffee House'—a teetotal club for working men with a capital of 100 £1 shares held by the men themselves. There were rooms for reading, smoking and bagatelle as well as skittle and quoit grounds, and a separate room for boys under fourteen who were not allowed to use the main rooms. The Aldridge Cricket Club, founded before 1874, has long been a source of parochial pride. It is still flourishing, as is also the Aldridge Hockey Club. August Bank Holiday Monday was a village occasion when every one who could visited the Horticultural Show which at one time was supported by foot races, followed later in the day by more frivolous contests and dancing. Both Horticultural Society and Hockey Club are indebted to Sir Cliff Tibbits, who permits them to use his grounds at Cedar Court. Other societies have also been allowed to avail themselves of his hospitality. He is the only Aldridge man of recent years to be knighted, but that honour was granted mainly for his services to Walsall where he is an alderman. During the difficult 1920's, when money was scarce and to work a short week was common, the Primitive Methodists at Leighswood catered for a real need by providing an Institute. There, cheaply, one could play billiards, tennis, badminton, table tennis or football, and there were frequent dances. For a short period in the 1930's four football teams were fielded, but two were more usual. The Institute was destroyed by fire in 1935, shortly before the Primitives and Wesleyans, who had then joined forces, opened the new church, Wesley Hall, in Anchor Road. Not until the 1930's could Aldridge boast of a cinema and save for the Assembly Rooms and the ex-Servicemen's Club, both privately owned, there is no public hall. After the First World War there was much talk about building a Memorial Hall, but all the talk came to nothing.

So many schools have sprung up in the Urban District during the last seventy or eighty years, that to trace their growth would be tedious. They range from boarding schools at both Beech Tree House and Bay Tree House to the fine new Primary School at Raeburn Road, Pheasey, and from the new school in Leighswood Avenue, built as a Primary School, but so far only used as a Secondary Modern, to the residential Druid Heath School of Dr. Barnardos. The latter, which uses premises originally built by the Royal Antediluvean Order of Buffaloes as an Orphanage (1920), is particularly interesting, receiving boys from all over the country, but during their stay here, endeavouring to link them with the life of the neighbourhood. Because of the speed with which the population has expanded, educational provision has tended to lag behind. Several large new schools have been promised, one of which is to be a Grammar School. For several years local parents have agitated for this, believing that insufficient Grammar Schools places for their children have been made available in other districts.

That is, perhaps, a good note on which to end this story, looking hopefully to the future. There also lies the maturity of Aldridge as an Urban District. The next decade may well be decisive as to whether the four villages with their flood of immigrants can be welded into a conscious community, an awareness which, to some degree, would enrich the lives of all future men of Aldridge.

BIBLIOGRAPHY

H.M.S.O. Census Returns.
List of Mines (1889-1936).
B.R.L., Representations to the Minister of Health as to the alteration of the boundaries of the Borough (Walsall, 29th Nov., 1920).
Eleventh Annual Report on the Health and Sanitary condition of the Walsall Rural Sanitary Authority (459127).
Walsall Free Press.
Finch Smith, *Notes & Collections of the Parish of Aldridge.*

APPENDIX I

SETTLEMENT AND FARMING IN THE PARISH OF ALDRIDGE (WEST MIDLANDS) PRIOR TO 1650

INTRODUCTION

From about 1200 to 1849 the parish of Aldridge consisted of the two townships of Aldridge and Great Barr as shown in fig. 1. Apart from an extensive mesolithic chipping floor[1] by the Bourne Brook, there is no evidence for any settlement within the parish boundaries during prehistoric times though the odd worked flint and three stone-axes have been found.[2] Despite the proximity of the Ryknield Street, there is a similar lack of evidence for settlement during the Roman period, save for a number of Roman coins with a brooch found near the parish boundary (Nat. Grid Ref. SK 0301) at the end of the 18th century,[3] followed by a billon tetradrachma (A.D. 287–8) found near the same place in 1957.[4] Air photographs have not revealed any crop-marks suggesting early settlement within this area which is now part if the West Midlands conurbation.

Evidence for Saxon settlement is also scarce. In view of the different types of settlement that emerged, the difference in name of the two townships is interesting: Barr is nonhabitative and British (Celtic — a summit): Aldridge is habitative and Saxon (Alrewic, the *wic* by the alders). A Saxon charter of 957 refers to a grant of Little Aston and Barr giving the bounds.[5] Unfortunately these cannot be identified on the ground save for part of the northern boundary that followed the Bourne Brook.[6] Domesday shows that by 1086 this estate had been split up with Little Aston becoming part of Shenstone whilst Magna Barr and Parva Barr were separated from each other. This happened before the Conquest since Domesday shows each part as having been held by different Saxons.

After the Conquest, both Great Barr and Aldridge were granted to William fitz Ansculf of Dudley Castle. They were joined to form the manor of Great Barr and Aldridge. Eventually Aldridge became a separate but subsidiary manor. When the parish church was built at

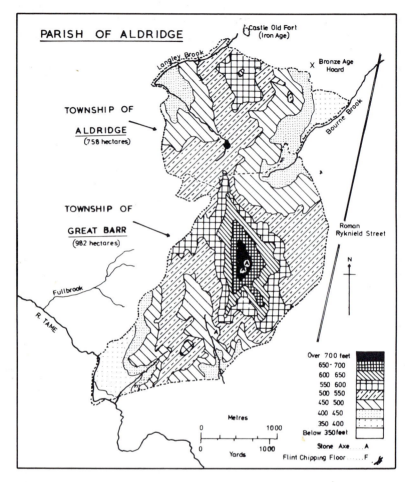

PARISH OF ALDRIDGE

Castle Old Fort
(Iron Age)

Longley Brook

Bronze Age
Hoard

TOWNSHIP OF
ALDRIDGE
(758 hectares)

Bourne Brook

TOWNSHIP OF
GREAT BARR
(982 hectares)

Roman
Ryknield Street

N

Fullbrook

R. TAME

Metres
0   1000

Yards
0   1000

Over 700 feet
650 - 700
600 650
550 600
500 550
450 500
400 450
350 400
Below 350feet

Stone Axe ....A
Flint Chipping Floor ......F

Fig. 1.   Aldridge Parish — Relief

Aldridge *c.*1200, Great Barr was included in Aldridge parish though it soon had its own chapel subsidiary to the parish church.

From the 11th century the whole parish was within the royal forest of Cannock. In 1125, Great Barr was disafforested and became part of a private chase — Sutton Chase, belonging to the Earl of Warwick. Aldridge was disafforested at the end of the 13th century, but unlike Great Barr did not become part of a private chase.[7]

GROWTH OF SETTLEMENT — ALDRIDGE (figs. 2 and 3)

Aldridge is divided into two parts by the geological fault which separates the heavy clay soils of the west from the light Bunter sands and gravels of the east. In due course meadow land and enclosed pastures were concentrated in the west, arable and common in the east.

The exact site of the first Saxon settlement that gave Aldridge its name is unknown. Both east and west were wooded originally and today woodland shrubs such as field maple and hazel are plentiful in the older hedges (and in some of the more recent ones too) on both types of soil. The name 'Aldridge', the *wic* by the alders, suggests a dairy farm near water (water is essential for alders to thrive) though *wic* does not always indicate dairying. The vicinity of Pool Green (fig. 3) where a number of roads meet and where there was a large pool, seems the most likely site. The pool was largely destroyed when the railway was built and the area is now fully built over. No archaeological finds suggesting Saxon occupation have been found there, nor for that matter anywhere else in Aldridge.

at Aldridge with land for three ploughs, an acre of meadow and woodland pasture five furlongs by three. Farming then was mixed. The arable developed in the light sandy area in the form of open or common fields. The earliest church terrier, 1684,[8] refers to the fields in their final stage of development and these are shown on fig. 3 at their greatest extent. The glebe in 1684 included 96 'ridges or buts'. Of these, 44 were in Drewed field, 27 in Brampthull field, 17 in Daniel field and 8 in Whetstone field. These were the main common fields. Roads ran into them as shown on the map, to give access, and three of these four roads still survive as dead ends, whilst the fourth, Whetstone Lane, has been extended only recently to join another

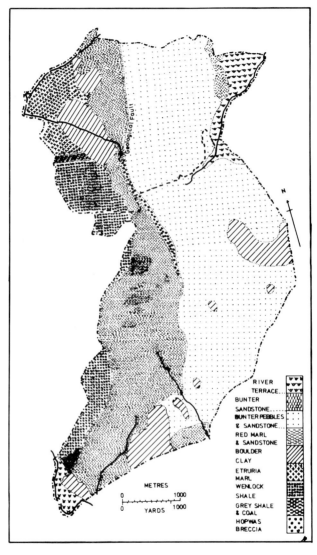

Fig. 2.   Aldridge Parish — Geology

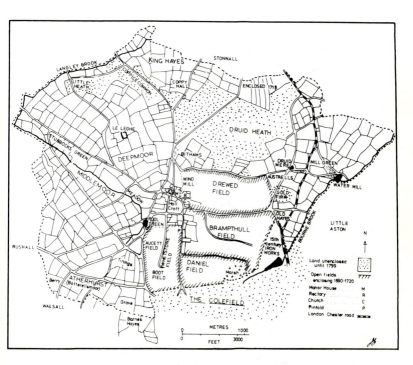

Fig. 3.   Aldridge Township — Settlement

road. Drewed field reached out to Gold Firm by the 17th century,[9] but the need for the much earlier Bithams enclosures suggests the field may have reached its full extent long before that. Brampthull field reached the border with Great Barr near to Bourne Pool by the end of the 15th century.[10] Daniel field also was limited by the Great Barr border. Whetstone field by the beginning of the 17th century not only reached its greatest extent, but had been divided into three, Whetstone field (eastern part), Aucett field (western part) and Boot field (southern part). These operated as a separate three-field system with its own manor court independent of the main manor of Aldridge. Some court rolls for this tiny manor survive in the County Record Office.[11] This unusual arrangement seems to have followed troubles in the Jordan family after their purchase of the main manor of Aldridge. A small, short-lived common field also began in the 17th century at Middlemoor.[12] The later field pattern suggests that this may have been on the south-western side of the patch of boulder clay shown on fig. 2. The area is now part of a large industrial estate.

Within the common fields were enclosures. The 1684 terrier mentions several when giving the boundaries of glebe strips. Others are mentioned in much earlier documents. Slade Croft and Scrivenors Yard are both said to have been in Brampthull field, though a different deed states Slade Croft was in Daniel field. The use of such enclosures is implied by the statement of Thomas Carm that on 17 August 1598 he mowed hay in Brampthull field with Thomas Boden until noon when it rained.[13] In 1583 it was recorded that Richard Scottesfield held a 'cottage, croft and certain closes of arable land in the common fields of Aldridge'.[14] Such enclosures cannot now be located by botanical means for most of the hedges have gone. Some that remain have been reduced to clumps of thorn linked with barbed wire, much of Drewed field is a golf-course, half Brampthull field is a huge sand quarry and part of the remainder are school playing-fields, whilst Whetstone field (all three parts) is entirely built over. The fact that enclosures within common fields were allowed at Aldridge reflects the extent of pasture available making the loss of an enclosure from the common pasture, when an open field was fallow, of less importance to the community generally. There was a shortage of arable by the 16th century as demonstrated by the fines levied in Great Barr courts on Aldridge men for ploughing on the Colefield.[15]

   Between the common fields and the heavy clays was the centre of the settlement. The manor-house or Old Hall (fig. 3, M) stood on a sandy site near the church. In the 17th century it consisted of hall, kitchen, parlour, buttery, cellar, bolting house, kitchen chamber, best chamber, first chamber and a cock-loft.[16] It has suffered several rebuildings since then. The church was built c. 1200[17] and until recently the rectory stood immediately north of the church, on the opposite side of the Green (the short road giving access to Drewed field — not the road now so-called). The 'town buts' were there.[18] This could be considered the name of the near strips or butts in Drewed field, but Shaw had access to a court roll which stated that the constable was ordered to set 'long shooting buts in their ancient and accustomed place'.[19] In the early 18th century part of this area was known as 'the play piece'.[20] The terrier of 1684 refers to the rectory as then being of five bays with nine bays of barning and other outbuildings, a foldyard, two gardens and two orchards. The rector farmed his glebe as well as collecting his tithes. An inventory shows the rectory had a hall, parlour, kitchen, buttery, parlour chamber, hall chamber, kitchen chamber, brew house, bolting house, dairy-house and two small rooms or cupboards, where books and valuables were kept, known as the study and the closet.[21] The rectory compared favourably with the manor-house. One rector, the Rev. John Scott (1575–1621)[22] was at that time the richest man in the parish, but an earlier rector, Philip Whildon (1544–56)[23] who lived during the religious troubles of the 16th century, died one of the poorest.

   Farm-houses clustered in the village centre and were still there last century (the Elms, Rookery Farm, Noddy Park Farm, Manor Farm, etc.). One large medieval cruck-house that stood on the High Street has recently been described in detail[24] though unfortunately it is not yet possible to connect the house with a particular family or landholding.

   Windmill field appears in undated extracts from medieval court rolls compiled for a 17th century brief.[25] There are many other 17th century references to Windmill field in deeds, etc. and a poster of 1801, describing land for sale, refers to 'the old windmill'. Tithe returns and the tithe map fix the position of Windmill field where there is still a large man-made mound presumably once used for a post-mill.

Meadow land adjoined Pool Green and its associated stream. The meadow was enclosed[26] not common meadow and stretched out towards Stubbocks Green.

The Domesday entry refers to but a small part of the later township. The area around the settlement must have been woodland for later medieval documents are full of references to woods, assarts and the clearance of woodland — all part of the royal forest in 1086 and as elsewhere not mentioned in the Domesday survey. The woods were gradually cleared giving way to moors and heaths which were later enclosed, but retaining 'moor' as an element in later field-names. No surviving Aldridge field name suggest Saxon enclosure. From 1086 to 1300 waste of woods within the forest area was a punishable offence. Records of fines imposed give some indication of where land was cleared in the 13th century. Some refer to clearances at Atherhurst[27] where woodland gave way to Botterellsmoor and by the 15th century to many enclosures. Some hedges there are botanically rich with six or seven different species of shrub per 30 yard stretch (for botanical dating see below).

At the end of the 12th century, Drogo of Aldridge was fined for a forest offence.[28] The diminutive of Drogo is Dru, hence his wood became the Druwode of medieval charters, later Drewed and then Druid, so that clearance there became Druid Heath. There are many 14th century reference to enclosures there and the name of King Hayes (like Old Hayes further south) indicates some of these medieval enclosures.[29] Coppy Hall was a medieval house destroyed this century but held in the 14th century by the Gorwey family.[30] The enclosures called Bithams date from that time too.[31] The enclosures of 1718 are marked on fig. 3, as their strip-like appearance might seem to indicate an earlier common field. In fact the enclosures were taken from Druid Heath in 1718 to endow the new Aldridge Free Grammar School. The shape of the fields may be due to the continued use of oxen then for ploughing. Alternatively the shape may reflect earlier, short-term enclosure. Cultivation of part of the common was permitted occasionally for four year stretches the land then returning to the common for at least seven years before again being ploughed.[32]

Land to the east, by Bourne Brook is alluvium and some was enclosed early; some hedges near the mill yield seven species of shrub per stretch. Here too the names of a number of fields include 'moor' suggesting some lapse between clearance and enclosure.

Druid Mere must have been very welcome for cattle on Druid Heath and also to drovers who could leave the near-by main road to feed and water their animals on the heath. The road by Druid Mere later was known as Drover's Lane. There are many references to drovers breaking into closes elsewhere in the parish from the 15th century onwards.[33] In the 17th century Dr. Plot reported that an abundance of water in Druid Mere was a certain sign of a poor harvest to come.[34]

The Austrells and land immediately east of it were enclosed before 1348[35] but some common remained at Gold Firm and only disappeared with the enclosure award of 1799.

On the opposite side of the township was the medieval moated house called 'Le Leghe'. Very little is known about this site which was destroyed last century by a colliery and a railway embankment. The earliest documentary evidence for it comes from 1388.[35] The name, a French form of the Saxon *leah* (meaning woodland or woodland clearance) need not indicate a Norman origin. In the 18th century it was a farm-house. By the 14th century trees in this area had not only been cleared but the resulting moor (Deepmoor) had given way to enclosed meadow.[36]

The Tinings was waste land until 1605 when William Wiggin received permission to erect a cottage there on the waste and presumably enclosed some of the land. At Berry was enclosed pasture.[37]

GROWTH OF SETTLEMENT — GREAT BARR (fig. 4)

The settlement pattern at Great Barr was very different to that at Aldridge. The only documentary reference to selions or strips is to a block of four that were bounded on two sides by roads and on each of the other two sides by land of one man only.[38] This was not part of an open-field system but rather a close cultivated in four ridges possibly to secure good drainage. If there ever was an open-field system here it had disappeared long before the time for which we

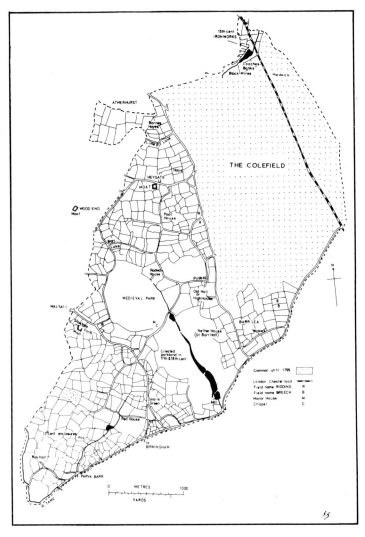

Fig. 4.   Great Barr Township — Settlement

have documentary evidence. The field pattern is against such a system ever having existed.

At Domesday Great Barr had but a small population (one villein and one bordar) but much woodland pasture (one league by four furlongs). Taken from Cannock Forest in 1125 it became part of Sutton Chase held by the earls of Warwick.[39] By the 13th century, the earl was allowing assarting and the cutting of underwood extensively.[40] At first this seems to have been especially at the south-western end of the town township, an area now covered by modern development but where the field pattern at the time of the tithe survey showed a mosaic of small irregular fields typical of woodland enclosures. The border here with Parva Barr was ill-defined.[41] The documentary references are not only to enclosures but also tenements in this area.[42]

The closes included woodland[43] as well as enclosing pasture and arable.[44] Some small patches of common land remained until the 17th century.[45] Other enclosures were near Atherhurst (referred to under Aldridge) where again the border was doubtful. Here several fields include 'hay' as an element in their names. Some woodland may have remained or else was replanted for there are 17th-century references to wood at Barnes Hays. One will of that date also refers to limestone-burning and the right of 'egress and regress' which perhaps explains Lime Pit Lane (fig. 4).[46] A case has also been stated for a lime-kiln somewhere in this area in Saxon times.[47] Medieval enclosure here was with ditch and dead hedge.[48] At Wood End, too, enclosures straddled the Great Barr border.[49] There also surviving hedges are botanically rich (six varieties of shrub per stretch).

The settlement seems to have had no real nucleus. The chapel built before 1257[50] adjoined the original manor-house (now Chapel Farm)[51] the road originally passing south of the church and not north of it as at present. Today there is no evidence for other medieval buildings in this vicinity though the creation of parkland to the south in the 17th and 18th centuries may have removed such evidence. Even in the 14th century some buildings were deliberately destroyed in adjoining Parva Barr[52] and the same forces could have been at work in Great Barr. Eventually there was a straggle of houses at Snails Green and elsewhere by the Walsall—Birmingham road. Shaw who consulted douments not now available claimed that one lord of the manor, Sir Robert Stapleton, lived at the moated site at Heygate.[53] Construction of such a site, fashionable in the 14th century, would be in accord with what is known of the man.[54] If enclosure there followed construction of the moat and did not precede it, it would explain why the near-by hedges are not quite so rich botanically (four or five species per stretch) as the hedges at Wood End and Atherhurst. It is to be noted though that two fields to the south-east (fig. 4) bear the name 'Ridding' which suggests Saxon clearance as do also the field-names near Barr Lea that include 'breech' (Saxon *brec*).

The medieval deer-park, by the chapel and manor-house, is first mentioned in 1335 when men were accused of breaking in and stealing.[55] As lords of the manor seldom resided in Great Barr from that date until the mid 16th century, it is nor surprising that the park was soon divided into six enclosed fields, later subdivided further.[56]

The sandy land stretching eastwards from the top of Barr Beacon was cleared by medieval charcoal-burners. From 1304 onwards there are many references to the 'Colefield'[57] which reached across to Little Aston and on to Sutton. The theft in 1323 of £200 from Elias the Collier from London[58] suggests that at that time charcoal burning here was on a large scale. Two hundred years later, the Colefield was just a big expanse of furze and heath.[59] The destruction of trees would lead to some leaching of the light soils. This, with the absence of water on the cold eastern slope of Barr Beacon may explain the lack of settlement until recent times. In the Middle Ages it was a lawless place where murders and robberies were committed.[60] Occasionally parts of the Colefield were ploughed by men from Aldridge as well as Great Barr.[61] The court roll of 15 March 1610/11 suggests that at that time one day's ploughing on the Colefield was permitted for each cottage in Great Barr. A later roll, 27 Oct. 1685, laid down rules for fencing, showing that parts of the Colefield then were at times converted into temporary common fields.

The ironworks on the fringe of the Colefield, belongs to the closing decades of the 15th century.[62] It consisted of a bloomery and a hammer-pond.

The name 'Hardwick' does not appear in documents until Elizabethan times. Since the Countess of Shrewsbury had held land at near-by Drayton, it is not impossible that the name came from that family. No early enclosures are known at this point and so no deductions are made from the place-name which, when occurring elsewhere, is taken to indicate a Saxon sheep-farm.

How far the Colefield stretched westwards is not certain. Probably it was no further than the crest of Barr Beacon as shown on fig. 4. Reference has already been made to the early enclosures near Heygate. Part of Barr Lea was enclosed by the 13th century[63] but, as this is now part of the Pheasey housing estate, one cannot check hedgerow dating there. The name Pheasey comes from Simon Vesey who in 1559 held a messuage there with 80 acres of arable, 12 of meadow, 3 of pasture, 3 of wood and 40 of furze and heath.[64] Radway House is mentioned in the will of Alice Scott (1588) though Alice who had inherited the house did not live there. It should not be confused with Radway Manor which is a timber-framed house erected in 1934 on a different though near-by site, using old materials. Pool House and Pinfold House are mentioned in the 17th century and could be earlier. When the Scots bought the manor of Great Barr, the Old Hall became in effect the manor-house. According to the inventory of William Scott (will proved 1577/8) the Old Hall, sometimes called the High House or Over House included hall, kitchen, parlour, buttery, maids' chamber, solar over each of the buttery, parlour, hall and kitchen, a bolting house, bakehouse, servants' chamber, stable, cote house, barn and wain house. His son's inventory (Thomas Scott, will proved 1616) shows alterations giving a chamber over a porch, a new parlour and a gallery. Nether House, probably so-called in contrast to Over House, also was large. In 1675 it included parlour, old parlour, day house, kitchen, buttery, best chamber, little chamber, cheese chamber, parlour chamber, Follows (a personal name?) chamber and a kiln house (Ric. Scott inventory, 1675). Later it was much altered to become the Great Barr Hall of the 19th and present century. There were other large houses in the early-enclosed south-western area. Such was Red House, the home of William Brasebrygge in 1541 (see will of Ric. Newman proved 1541). At Ray Hall lived relatives of the Stamford family who owned half the manor in the later medieval period.

Great Barr was a township of scattered farms, some of them large, with a big expanse of heath to the east and enclosed fields of arable, pasture and meadow to the west — a division which again reflects the geological differences shown in fig. 2.

BOTANICAL DATING[65]

Botanical dating in this parish is not entirely satisfactory. In all 151 hedgerow counts were made. There is evidence in the field to suggest some mixed planting of hedges. Also there are hedges consisting only of hawthorn with a few bushes of field maple — a shrub normally only found in old, botanically-rich hedges. Even away from industrial and housing estates many of the hedges are in a bad state. Some of this appears to be due to land being over-grazed by horses who eat hedgerow shrubs. Where hedges remain, often woodland herbs, bluebells, wood anemonies, etc. which were present in the same hedges fifty years ago (boyhood memories), have now departed like the chaffinches, snipe and newts before them. Sometimes there is but polythened rubbish and sadness.

FARMING 1533–1643

There is insufficient documentary evidence for a worthwhile survey of medieval farming in the parish. The one surviving 12th century deed emphasizes the importance of pigs in the surrounding woods.[66] Medieval court rolls were assembled in a dispute between the lords of the two manors in the early 17th century. The briefs for each side containing extracts from the rolls, have survived[67] but the court rolls have not been seen since. One can say that money rents had been substituted for services by the 14th century, that the Great Barr court met every third week and at times dealt with Aldridge matters including those arising from the open fields and that at other times such matters were dealt with by the Aldridge court. Apart from that, there is little other than what has already been said about enclosures etc. The picture changes in the 16th century when another type of evidence becomes available. For the 110 years following 1533, 39 wills and 48 inventories have survived for Aldridge men and 36 wills and 46 inventories for Great Barr men. In all these relate to 100 parishioners. They include some of the very poor as well as richer people and are fairly evenly spread throughout the period except for an increase in 1597 and 1598 but those inventories do not suggest food shortage as was the case elsewhere at that time. On the muster roll for 1539,[68] 55 men are named for Aldridge and Great Barr. Details have survived for 16 of these suggesting that we have information for about one man in every three or four. This is sufficient to give a picture of farming here and to contrast in some respects open-field Aldridge with non-nucleated Great Barr. Further, the wills and inventories were usually written by either the curate of Great Barr or by the curate of Aldridge. As the resident rector of Aldridge controlled both men, policy in writing wills and inventories would not have differed much between the townships.

Farming was mixed and even the craftsmen were primarily farmers. The documents relate to rectors, millers, smiths, a weaver, a tailor, a wheelwright and a silver spurrier; they all farmed. Of 48 Aldridge inventories, 40 list at least one cow. Of the remaining eight, one was lord of the manor, five were living with other people and were not heads of households (witnessed by the absence of equipment relating to the fire and to cooking), one left cows in his will not included on the inventory and the eighth relates to a farmer, heavily in debt, who had been selling his stock. Thus virtually every household owned a cow reflecting the plentiful common and meadow. The position at Great Barr was similar. Of the 46 inventories, two relate topeople living with others and 43 of the other 44 include at least one cow. Some had up to 26 cows and heifers so that dairy produce was obviously marketed. Butter must have been sent to market immediately it was made for it appears only on five Aldridge and six Great Barr inventories and then in small amounts except for two gallons on one inventory, three pots and two lots of four pots on others. A pot held about 14 lb. Cheese-making equipment appears frequently but cheese itself is only mentioned on five Aldridge and seven Great Barr inventories. Thomas Cox of Aldridge with 31 cheeses is the only person who seems to have made cheese on any scale. Oxen were the draught animals; 15 Aldridge inventories include them usually in teams of four or six. They appear on 25 Great Barr inventories. Only one inventories, two relate to people living with others and 43 of the Some people hired others to plough and cart for them as is shown by debts for these services recorded as outstanding at the time of death. Numbers of young beasts suggest beef production. In all, apart from cows, heifers and oxen, 25 Aldridge men owned 172 calves and other cattle whilst 37 Great Barr men owned 294. Sheep were also important. For Aldridge 33 inventories refer to two or more sheep

(2,987 in total) whilst the 42 Great Barr inventories mentioning sheep give a total of 2,538. Wool is seldom mentioned, presumably being sold soon after shearing. The exception is that of the rector, the Rev. John Scott who had 60 stone of wool on hand at his death in 1621. His was the largest flock (320 sheep) but some wool may have come from tithes. Sheep were obviously regarded as wealth. In many wills, a ewe or a lamb were left to grandchildren and god-children in a manner reminiscent of the way Victorians opened bank accounts for children. Lambs are seldom distinguished from other sheep. They appear only sixteen times, the earliest inventory being dated 3 April. The inventories mention 155 lambs but as the same inventories refer to 871 other sheep (including wethers and 'hogges') the fertility rate does not seem very high. Nevertheless the sheep were increasing in importance against cattle as the following figures show:

Total value as shown on inventories:

	ALDRIDGE		GREAT BARR	
	Cattle	*Sheep*	*Cattle*	*Sheep*
1533–1600	£274	£94	£337	£108
1601–1643	£316	£243	£418	£245

Horses were also kept. Thirty-two Aldridge and thirty-three Great Barr inventories mention 182 horses. Of these, 41 were colts or fillies, 86 mares, 11 nags, 2 proper horses, 4 pack-horses, 18 caples, one gelding and 19 are just called horses. The caples are all on inventories before 1600. Their comparative value was small. They were probably small horses used for general purposes like the Irishman's donkey.

Of the 43 Aldridge inventories representing households, 17, mainly those of labourers, had no poultry, 21 people had hens, 15 had geese, 2 had ducks and one had turkeys. Five just used the general term 'poultry'. Of the 43 Great Barr inventories referring to households, 13 have no mention of poultry, 7 just use the general term poultry, 19 list hens, 17 list geese, 4 list ducks, 3 list turkeys and strangest of all, 5 including that of a blacksmith, list peacocks. The maximum number of hens kept was 13 though three or four was more usual. No one had more than 6 geese. Hence eggs and poultry were not being produced in quantity for the market. Only four Aldridge men and six of Great Barr had bees, but of these one man had eleven and another man six stalls (hives).

Pigs were kept by most people except the poorest; 25 Aldridge men had 87½ pigs whilst 35 Great Barr men had 176. These figures include a number of piglets. Whenever inventories mention food — and few do — they usually refer to flitches of bacon 'in the roof'; one refers to two flitches of beef there also; none mention mutton.

The Final Concords for Great Barr[69] often refer to free common of pasture for cattle but those for Aldridge [70] usually refer to free common of pasture for sheep. Many of the enclosed fields were of pasture. This is understandable especially for fattening and where oxen were used. After a day's work oxen cannot be turned on to well-grazed common if more work is required the following day; enclosed pasture was essential for these animals. Commons were also used for fuel, turf and peat, and these were often cut on the Colefield especially near Black Mires.[71] Reference has already been made to ploughing on the waste and two Great Barr inventories refer to corn 'growing on the heath'.[72] The will of Thomas Smith (proved 1590/1) refers to a fine of 3*d*. per sheaf due from corn growing on pasture at Great Barr suggesting some concern for the quantity of grass available at that time.

It is difficult to assess the importance of corn against livestock. With the advent soon after harvest of Michaelmas and the need to pay rents then, much corn was probably sold as soon as possible. Unthrashed corn, like hay, was stored in barns by even the poorest. There is no mention of cornricks and only one mention of a haystack. Growing corn is referred to in inventories as being of so many acres or of so many days' (work). Thrashed corn is always indoors, usually in a dry upper chamber, to appear on the inventories mixed with beds and bedding. Usually no distinction is made between the various crops. Those that do, show 13 Aldridge men with a total of 22¼ days, 2 butts, 18 strikes, and 2½ thraves of rye; four men with 4 days, 4 acres and 20½ strikes of barley, bere or malt; ten men had 27 days, 4 acres and 7 strikes of oats; two men had five days of peas. Only one man grew wheat (1½ days); three men grew dredge; one man had 1½ days of French wheat and barley and one man had half a day of oats and vetches. The figures for Great Barr are 21 men had 35½ days, 1 close, 41 acres, 36 thraves, 48 strikes and 1 bushel of rye; 14 men had 38½ days, 6 thraves, and 17 strikes of oats; 9 men had 6 acres, 33 thraves and 11 strikes of barley, bere or malt; 1 man had three days of peas; 1 man 2 acres of French wheat and 4 men had 2 days and 22 acres of wheat. Save for slightly more wheat and barley with a little less oats, the heavy clay enclosed fields of Great Barr were producing the same crops as the light sandy open-fields of Aldridge. No one grew beans. Prices varied considerably throughout the period but where an inventory gives separate prices for the different crops it is clear that one day of rye was worth two days of oats and that a day of barley was worth only two thirds of a day of rye.

There seems to have been a growing appreciation of dung. It first apears on inventories in 1553 when 13 loads were valued at one shilling.[73] After 1578 such entries become common. It is often described as 'muck about the house' which raises the question of sanitation. This is especially so since only three inventories mention chamber-pots, one a close-bucket and none refer to close-stools or commodes.

It is possible that small amounts of hemp and flax were grown in gardens. Only one inventory mentions hempseed and linseed but 26 mention slippings of hemp, knickins or runtches of hemp, hempen yarn, towe or the like showing that hemp was spun in households, whilst one mentions a 'rypple combe' and three mention 'hetchells' (tools used for dealing with hemp). Thirteen inventories mention dressed flax or flax yarn. Only 24 of the lists include spinning-wheels and those were not for the poorest households although they were only valued at between one shilling and two shillings each. Some may still have used distaff and spindle for spinning.

The Great Barr manor court rolls that have survived for 1610 and 1612 show that much land was copyhold. Heriot was paid on inheritance of land or when land was sold to another person. The wills often refer to leases but give little detail since land was often already transferred to sons or dealt with by marriage settlements. What references there are show that leases were for long periods; sufficiently long for young children to grow up and for there still to be some years of the lease to run.

Although Aldridge was a nucleated village with open fields on light sandy soil, whereas Great Barr was non-nucleated with enclosed arable on heavy soil, farm products were almost identical. It must be asked which was the more efficient. The following figures are offered for comparison.

	ALDRIDGE (48 inventories)		GREAT BARR (46 inventories)	
	Total value	Average per person	Total value	Average per person
Cattle	£590	£12.3	£755	£16.4
Sheep	£337	£7.0	£353	£7.7
All livestock	£1,059	£22.1	£1,231	£26.7
All pertaining to farming including ploughs, etc.	£1,492	£31.1	£1,565	£34.0
Value of household chattells	£371	£7.7	£518	£11.3
Household chattells as percentage of farm goods	25%		33%	

Averages may be weighted by the very large or the very small so that sometimes the median gives a clearer picture. Ignoring sums included on some inventories for leases or debts which are omitted from other inventories, the median for Aldridge is that of J. Hopkys. He lived in a house with hall and parlour downstairs and with a chamber over each. He also had an 'old house' where there were two spinning-wheels, kneading trough, barrels and the like. He slept in the parlour where there were a bedstead, featherbed and bed-clothes with painted cloths that probably hung on the wall. Cooking was done in the hall where was the only chair in the house together with two forms and three stools. The chamber over the hall contained thrashed wheat, oats, barley and malt as well as a flock bed and bedding. The chamber over the parlour had two bedsteads, two mattresses, wool cards, scythe, etc. In the fields on 26 April, 1583, he had two days of rye, two days of oats, 1½ days of wheat (the only Aldridge man known to have grown it). He owned four cows, two heifers, one

yearling calf, three young calves, two horses, two mares, thirty-six
ewes, wethers and hogges, fourteen ewes with lambs, one pig and
two hens. He had no oxen and as he had neither plough, harrow nor
cart, he probably did not use his horses for draught purposes. His
only farm tools were a scythe, mattock, bill, shovel and a spade. He
owned various pieces of pewter but used wooden trenchers and had
two flitches of bacon and two flitches of beef 'in the roof'. His goods
were worth £21. 18s. 10d.

The median for Great Barr is the inventory of John Shelfield. With
a wife, two sons and two daughters, he lived in a house with hall and
parlour downstairs and one chamber upstairs over the parlour. He
too cooked in the hall where there were three chairs, a trestle-table
and a form. He had eleven platters, eight pewter dishes and six
saucers but no wooden trenchers. In the parlour were two bedsteads,
a feather bed and painted cloths 'about the bed', a store of bedding
(including twelve pairs of sheets), various barrels, churns, etc. In the
chamber were two bedsteads, two flock beds, a tirle bed, a coffer and
other odds and ends. He owned a wain body and new wheels for it,
three yokes, a harrow, four oxen, four cows, three young beasts,
two calves, a mare, a sow with three piglets, thirty-eight sheep,
twelve lambs, six geese, four hens, three capons and four ducks. On
3 July 1588 he had no thrashed corn on hand but had in the fields
three and a half days of rye, one and a half days of bere and four days
of oats. Exceptionally he also had the wool from thirty-eight sheep
with an unspecified quantity of butter and cheese. His goods were
worth £32. 3s. 4d. He owed £1 19s. 0d. and was owed £2 15s. 7d.
including 12d. for 1¾ days ploughing and another 12d. for 'carrying
coles'. For these no doubt he had used his ox-team.

However one looks at it, it appears that Great Barr farmers had the
edge over those of Aldridge. During the following century the open
fields of Aldridge disappeared after much buying and selling of strips
by private arrangement, well illustrated by deeds now in the County
Record Office.[74]

NOTE

All wills and inventories referred to are in the Lichfield Joint Record
Office. I am indebted to the staff of that office for courteous help in

finding the large number of documents consulted. The field boundaries shown in figs. 3 and 4 are based on the tithe map of Aldridge parish, 1840. The following abbreviations have been used:

BM   British Museum
BRL   Birmingham Reference Library
CRO   County Record Office, Stafford
SHC   *Staffordshire Historical Collections*
WSL   William Salt Library, Stafford

REFERENCES

1. A. Saville, 'Reconsideration of the prehistoric flint assemblage from Bourne Pool', *Trans*. xiv for 1972–73 (1973), pp. 6–28.
2. F. W. Shotton, Stone Implements of Warwickshire, *Trans. Birmingham Archaeol. Soc.*, lviii for 1934 (1937), p. 46.
    N. Thomas, Three pre-Roman Antiquities, *Trans. Birmingham Archaeol. Soc.*, lxxvii for 1959(1961), pp. 1–4.
    Proc. of Soc. of Antiquaries of London, 2nd Ser. vii (1876), p. 268.
3. S. Shaw, *hist. and Ant. of Staff* 1(1798), p. 35.
4. Found by a Mr. Williams who then resided at 5 York Road, Rushall. Identified by BM.
5. C. R. Hart, *Early Charters of Northern England* (1975), p. 94.
6. This is despite Rune Forsberg, 'Old English *ad* in English Place-Names', *Namn och Bygd*, lvii (Uppsala, 1970), pp. 20–82.
7. J. Gould, 'Food, Foresters Fines & Felons', *Trans*. vii for 1965–66 (1967), p. 23 and 38.
8. WSL MS.D120/a/PC/313.
9. Ibid.
10. BM Add.MS.24822, f.3.
11. CRO MS.3005/219.
12. Scott Charters 75 & 83, BRL 608953 & 608962.
13. For Slade Croft see CRO. MS. 3005/34; Tithe map and tithe returns in Lichfield Joint Record Office. For Thos. Carm, see Quarter Sessions, 40–41 Elizabeth, *SHC 1935* (1936), p. 163.
14. WSL. MS. D634A/3, p. 4.
15. Ibid.
16. Inventory John Jordan, will proved 1671.
17. J. Gould, 'Observations at Aldridge Church', *Trans.*, xviii for 1976/77 (1977), pp. 49–52.
18. Terrier 1684, CRO. MS.D120/A/PC/313.
19. S. Shaw, *Hist. and Ant. of Staffs*. ii(1801), p. 99.

20. Indenture 6 Aug. 1718. Thos. Cooper's grant of land for a charity school at Aldridge.
21. Inventory Gamaliel Pretty, will proved 1674.
22. Inventory J. Scott, will proved 1621.
23. Inventory P. Whildon, will proved 1556.
24. S. R. Jones & V. F. Penn, 'Medieval Cruck-trussed House in High Street, Aldridge', *Trans.* xviii for 1976/77 (1977), pp. 1–23.
25. BM Add. MS.24822, f. 4.
26. W. Fowler-Carter, Deeds in possession of Mr. Fowler, *Mid. Record Soc.* ii(1899), p. 153.
27. Major-Gen. Hon. G. Wrottesley, 'Pleas of the Forest', *SHC* v, pt. 1 (1884), p. 153.
28. Pipe Roll 2 John.
29. BM Add.MS., 24822, f. 3; Scott Charter 35, BRL 608903; etc.
30. S. R. Jones, 'Shelfield Lodge Farm', *Trans.* x for 1968/69 (1969), p. 69.
31. BM Add.MS. 24822, f. 3 & 4.
32. Great Barr manor court roll, 2 Oct. 1612.
33. e.g. *De Banco* Rolls 10 Henry VI, SHC xvii (1896), p. 142; 17 Henry VI, *SHC* New Ser. iii (1900), p. 147.
34. R. Plot, *Nat. Hist. of Staffordshire* (1686), Ch. 2, para. 29.
35. Scott Charter, BRL 608917.
36. Ibid. Also BM Add.MS. 24822, f. 3.
37. For Tinings, see Quarter Session Rolls 1605, *SHC 1940* (1940), p. 239. For Berry see, WSL. MS.D634A/30, p. 4.
38. Scott Charter 16, BRL 608894.
39. J. Gould, op. cit. in note 7.
40. [A. Bracken], *Forest and Chase of Sutton Coldfield* (1860), p. 35.
41. *Close Rolls (1237–1242)*, p. 237.
42. Scott Charters 10, 84, 86, 116, BRL 608888, 608963, 608964, 608993.
43. e.g. *De Banco* Rolls, 33 Ed. III, *SHC* xii, pt. 1 (1891), p. 172; 17–18 Ric. II, *SHC* xv (1894), p. 64; etc.
44. e.g. *De Banco* Roll, 3 Henry V, *SHC* xvii (1896), p. 54; etc.
45. Great Barr manor court roll, 15 March 1610.
46. John Jordan, will proved 1660.
47. Rune Forsberg, op cit. in note 6.
48. Major-Gen. Hon. G. Wrottesley, op. cit. in note 27, p. 165.
49. Scott Charter 38, BRL 608916; *De Banco* Roll, 18 Ric. II, *SHC* xv (1894), p. 66.
50. *Close Rolls (1256–1259)*, p. 145.
51. Scott Charters 84, 86, 116, BRL 608963, 608964, 608993.
52. *De Banco* Roll, 50 Ed. III, *SHC* xiii (1892), p. 131. A medieval homestead site has been claimed at Nat. Grid Ref. SP 04789552 but the present writer is unconvinced.
53. S. Shaw, op. cit. in note 19, p. 98.
54. See p. 25–6 above.
55. *De Banco* Roll, 9 Ed. III, *SHC* xi (1890), p. 62.

56. Scott Charter 84, BRL 608963.

57. Cal. of Final Concords, *SHC 1911* (1911), p. 61; etc.

58. *Coram Rege* Roll, 17 Ed. II, SHC x (1889), p. 46. For Confirmation see Magnum Registrum Album, doc. 701, *SHC 1924* (1926), p. 335.

59. Cal. of Final Concords, *SHC* xiii (1892), pp. 296–7.

60. e.g. *Coram Rege* Roll, 17 Ed. II, *SHC* x (1889), pp. 46–7.

61. WSL MS.D634A/30, pp. 3 & 4.

62. J. Gould, 'Excavation of 15th Cent. Iron Mill', *Trans.* xi for 1969–70 (1971), pp. 58–63.

63. BM Add.MS. 24822, f. 2.

64. Cal. of Final Concords, *SHC* xiii (1892), pp. 235–6.

65. Dr. Hooper's hypothesis is that each different species of shrub present in a 30 yard stretch of hedgerow indicates an age of approximately 100 years. See M. D. Hooper's *et al. Hedges and Local History* (1971), pp. 6–13.

66. CRO 3005/1.

67. WSL MS. D634A/30; BM Add.MS. 24822.

68. Muster roll of Staffs., 1539, *SHC* New Ser. iv (1901), p. 95.

69. Cal. of Final Concords, *SHC* xvi (1895), pp. 150, 221, 225; etc.

70. Cal. of Final Concords, *SHC* xiv (1893), p. 192; *SHC* xv (1894), p. 130; etc.

71. BM Add.MS. 24822, f 3; etc.

72. Thomas Smith, will proved 1590/1; Ric. Dutton, will proved 1606.

73. Ric. Shelfield, will proved 1553.

74. Especially papers under reference 3005.

APPENDIX II

THE QUESTION is frequently asked about the arms and crest of Aldridge: no arms or crest has ever been officially granted to the district, but the Urban District Council use the crest that was granted to the Scott family.

Of the many families in England with the surname 'Aldridge' or 'Aldrich', as the name of the village was once spelt, a few have had arms and crests granted. These may or may not have been descended from people of this village, but at the time arms were granted, they had then no known ties with Aldridge. The village is only known to have given its name to one prominent family, that of 'de Alrewych', who lived here in the thirteenth and fourteenth centuries; they did not, as far as is known, bear arms.

The first mention of the Scott arms is in the Visitation of 1663. The arms of Thomas Scott of Great Barr were then recorded as being

'Argent, on fesse gules cottized azure, between three catherine wheels sable, as many lambs passant of the field. Crest: a beacon sable, fired proper, ladder gules.'

A white (or silver) shield with a broad horizontal red band edged in blue on which were three lambs. Above the band were two black catherine wheels and one below the band. The crest was a black beacon, flaming, with a red ladder. See S.H.C. II (2); and Harleian Soc. Vol. 1912, p. 67.

PLATES

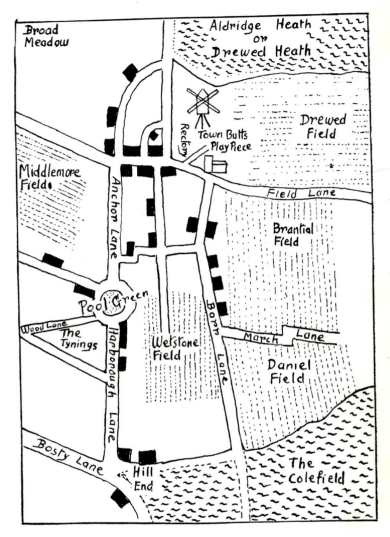

17th century Aldridge showing the open fields.

Compiled from Terriers etc. The site of the windmill is doubtful. The roads named Field Lane, Barr Lane, March Lane, Wood Lane and Harborough Lane are now Little Aston Road, Erdington Road, Daniel Lane, Walsall Road and Birmingham Road respectively. Many cottages were of thatched limestone.

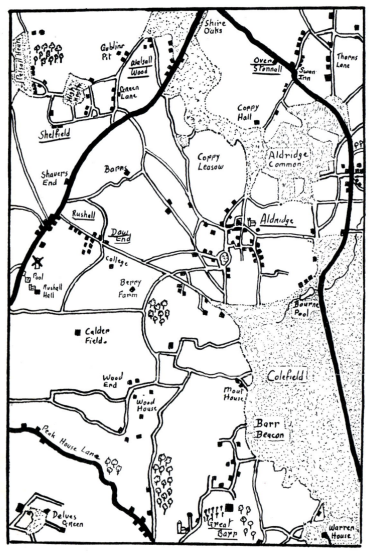

18th century Aldridge (based on Yates Survey of 1769).

━━━━ Turnpike road.　　▨▨▨ Unenclosed common.

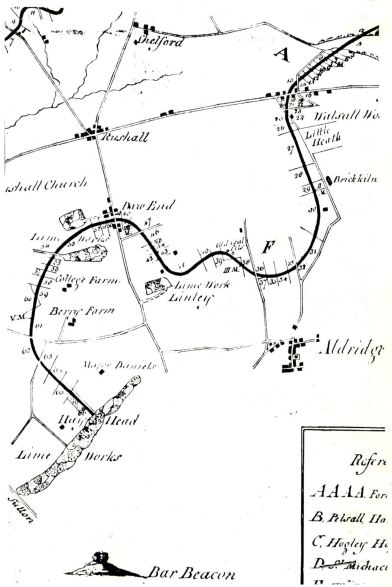

Part of the survey made 1792–3 for the extension of the Wyrley and Essington Canal showing the Limeworks and 'Old Coal Pits'.

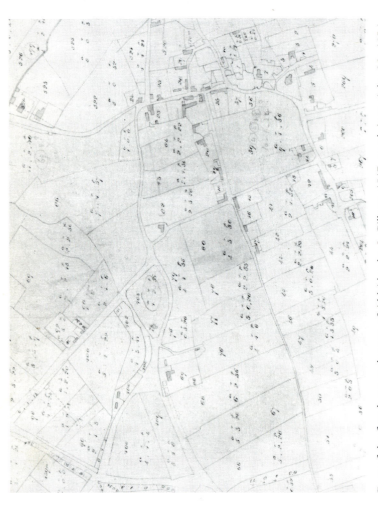

Part of the first large-scale map of Aldridge by J. Gilbert, 1817, north is to right. No.105 is Pool Green, No.1 is the Manor House, No.4 is the Grammar School.

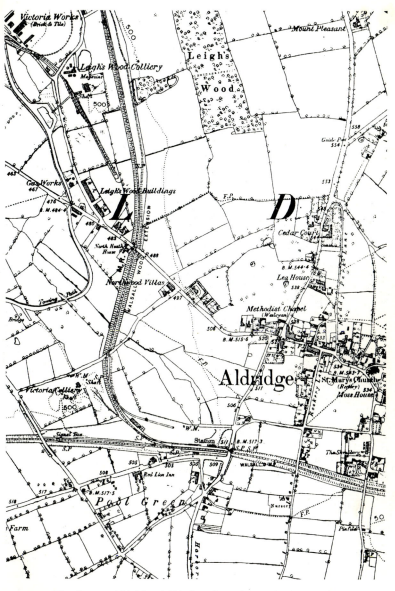

North east Aldridge 1834 (based on the Ordnance Survey)

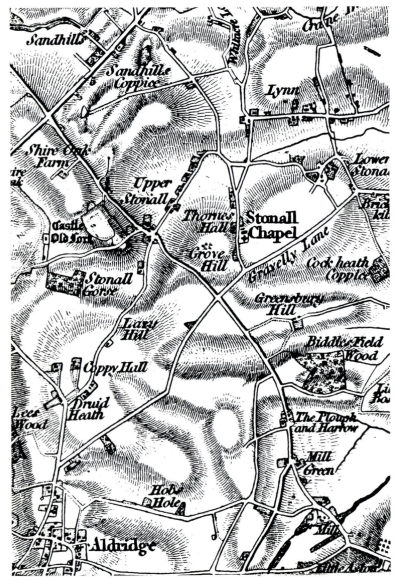

Aldridge 1882–5 (based on the Ordnance Survey)

High Street, Aldridge

High St. Aldridge facing west about 1925. The cruck-house is on the extreme left. All buildings shown have now been demolished.

(from the John Sale Collection).

High St. Aldridge facing east about 1925, showing the drinking fountain and horse trough. All buildings shown have now been demolished.

(from the John Sale Collection).

Aldridge Church about 1800.

(from J. Finch Smith, Notes and Collections, part 2, 1889).

Aldridge Church about 1930.

Aldridge Free Grammar School, 1847, drawing by I. Buckler.
(by permission of the trustees of the William Salt Library).

ALDRIDGE
FREE GRAMMAR
SCHOOL.

Fellow Inhabitants!

    THE Day is fast approaching when it will be your duty to shew once more your numerical strength in defence of the Rights and Intellectual Interests of your Children and your Children's Children. Too long has the Aldridge Free Grammar School been conducted upon an Useless and Inefficient System. Too long has the Education of your Children been neglected, and the Funds belonging to your Charity, in part, misappropriated. The single act of giving £40. per annum out of the Funds of this Charity to an individual sufficiently exhibits the abuse which exists: because, for what is it given? Not as a reward of his services. Not as a reward for his able manner of Teaching; nor for the great proficiency the boys had made under his Instruction: but as a compromise for his Insulting and Agravating Behaviour to the present *Acting Trustees*, when they (being completely tired by the frequent complaints of the inhabitants) thought fit to give him notice of dismissal. This glaring instance of *Ignorance* of *Duty and Power* or *Mismanagement*, on the part of the present Self-elected Trustees must alone be sufficient to prove to you the necessity of Reform in the management of the Charity. But although depriving you, the Inhabitants and Interested Parties, to whom belong the Moneys and Funds of this Charity) of £40 every year which ought to be spent in the Education of your Children, may be considered *a great Evil and Fraud*: yet, other Evils of nearly equal magnitude, are, at the present time, in existence.

    Is not the System of Education practised in the School, in the present moment, such as is of very little use to the Scholars? Are your Children receiving an Education which will fit them for any situation, even in the middle classes of Society; such an Education as the Reverend Founders no doubt intended for them. If you will look into the different Charities in many parts of England, particularly upon the borders of Scotland, you will find that there are common occurrences of Youth being fitted for the professions of either *Law, Physic*, or *Divinity*; and this, be it understood, at Schools which are supported by funds from £40 *to* £100 *per annum*—Fellow Inhabitants! mark the contrast: you have a School, the funds of which amount to nearly £150 *per annum*, and can you boast of any children who have received an education at this School to fit them for any of these professions? Have any of them received a common education, sufficient even for a tradesman? I defy the Trustees or the Master to produce one person who has received an education in this School, which will fit him for the situation of School-master, or even a Manufacturer's Clerk. No; fellow-inhabitants, such is the *wretched, miserable, deceptive System* practised, that while surrounding parishes are making rapid progress in intellectual knowledge; nay, while in England and the rest of Europe the people are improving their minds and cultivating their understanding—are banishing the degrading Delusions of Ignorance and Superstition, and are basking in the rays of Intellectual Light— this Parish remains plunged in the scanty stock of Intellectual Knowledge which generally existed in the seventeenth century. To what is this state of the Parish to be attributed? Not to its poverty or want of means, for there is scarcely a place in the Empire, of equal size and local situation, better provided with the means of Education, than this Parish. It must be evident to you, then, that the fault rests in the *mismanagement of the Conductors* of this charity. ON WEDNESDAY NEXT there will be an opportunity for you to place the future management of the School upon a much better and more profitable footing; if you conceive that a good Education for your Children is worth your consideration, every individual so interested will not fail to attend the meeting, *by half-past ten o'clock*. You will, then, by your attendance nd conduct on that day, insure for your children, and their posterity for ever, a good and seful Education.

Charles Juxon.

Aldridge, February 25th, 1833

A typical Juxon broadside.

Great Barr Hall (Nether House), 1868.
(by permission, from the Sir Benjamin Stone Collection, Birmingham Public Libraries).

The Old Hall, Great Barr.

Cruck-house High St., Aldridge under demolition, 1965.

Blacksmith's forge, Pool Green, about 1925, with the last blacksmith, Mr. Pointon.

(by permission Miss E. Pointon).

Aldridge railway station about 1908. Now demolished.

(from the John Sale Collection).

Leighswood Colliery about 1925.

(from the John Sale Collection).

INDEX

INDEX

Bold figures refer to Maps and Illustrations facing page indicated.